FLOYD S. SPENCE

EXCEED YOURSELF

How to unlock your greatness and live your best life possible

Copyright © 2018 Floyd Spence.

All rights reserved. No part of this book may be used or reproduced by any means, graphic, electronic, or mechanical, including photocopying, recording, taping or by any information storage retrieval system without the written permission of the publisher except in the case of brief quotations embodied in critical articles and reviews.

Cover: Daryl Anderson, Sr.
Interior Page design & layout: OA.Blueprints, LLC
Editor: Averil Kurtz
Photography: Profex Images

Printed in the United States of America

978-0-692-16442-6

Contents

INTRODUCTION.. 1

PART ONE: THERE'S GREATNESS WITHIN YOU

CHAPTER

1. THE POWER OF HUNGER.. 8
2. THE PSYCHOLOGY OF SUCCESS................................. 16
3. UNLOCK YOUR GREATNESS..................................... 27

PART TWO: IT'S POSSIBLE

CHAPTER

4. TUNE INTO YOUR PURPOSE.................................... 46
5. LET YOUR PASSION FUEL YOU................................. 57
6. GETTING YOUR DREAM OFF THE LAUNCHING PAD.......... 74

PART THREE: NO LIMITS

CHAPTER

7. BEATING THE ODDS.. 86
8. PUSH YOURSELF TO THE NEXT LEVEL......................... 112
9. SO WHERE DO I GO FROM HERE?............................. 128

GLOSSARY... 133
NOTES.. 137
BIBLIOGRAPHY.. 142
ABOUT THE AUTHOR... 153

DEDICATION

To the memory
of my parents,
Theophilus and Alma Spence

ACKNOWLEDGEMENTS

I am grateful to the many people who have helped me make writing this book possible. First, I would like to thank my "superhero" dad who worked very hard to ensure that his family was taken care of. He was my role model for honesty, integrity, and hard work. Thanks, also, to my mother who taught me to love unconditionally and how to believe and expect more of myself.

I would also like to thank my family: my two children, Akilah and Jadon, who believed in me and provided me with a great source of strength and encouragement during the process of writing this book. Thanks to my amazing wife Lisa, my partner in marriage, struggles, and triumphs. Without her love and support, this book would not have become a reality. Thanks to my siblings for the support I have received on my journey towards personal and professional achievement these many years.

Thanks to the hard working men and women whom I met in the Canadian Armed Forces—people who taught me the value of commitment, hard work, team effort, and the importance of not quitting, even when we feel like it. I am immensely grateful to Dr. John Maxwell and the teaching faculty of the John Maxwell Team, for adding value to me through mentorship and the personal and professional development lessons I have been taught, over the past couple of years.

A special thanks to my primary editor, Mrs. Averil Kurtz, whose insightful reading of my work has proven to be invaluable. Finally, thanks to those of you who read this book and pass it on to a friend, relative, or just anyone you believe needs it for inspiration. I strongly believe that if more of us follow our purpose and work hard in living the best life possible, we could make this world a better one today and for generations to come.

INTRODUCTION

Who is Floyd Spence, and why did he write this book?

There's greatness within you! Everyone of us, is gifted with the seed of greatness at birth. We are all born with a gift—the potential to make an impact and a big difference in this world. "I can't believe it's you!" he remarked with a look of surprise and shock on his face. "Are you the same guy who used to hang around outside my classroom wasting time while school was in progress?" he asked. "Yes!" I replied, flashing a smile of contentment as I wait with elation and eager anticipation to explain how my life had changed.

This was a conversation I had with a former high school friend of mine during an event I attended in Toronto, Canada, some years ago. Travis, who was my junior in high school, knew of my struggles during my high school years and was surprised to see how much my life had changed over the years. So who was that Floyd that Travis knew and who is this Floyd that he just met? Let's find out!

For the first four years in high school, I was a failure. I hadn't had a single grade above a C and most of my grades were somewhere between a C- and an F. As a matter of fact, my academic performance was so poor that I had to repeat the tenth grade. Behaviorally, things weren't that great either. I was suspended three times in two years and was about to be expelled during my first year in the tenth grade when a mother's love saved me from being a High School drop-out.

Pandemonium had broken out in the classroom! It was a couple of weeks before Christmas and our teacher had stepped out for a few minutes to take care of some important business. The moment she stepped out, a few of us turned the classroom into a "bashment party." Len, my close friend provided the sound track with his booming voice-box that commanded the attention of the room, while I sang some of the latest dancehall and R & B songs, to the elation of our rowdy classmates who cheered us along.

After entertaining the masses for a while, we ran out of songs, but I decided to take the entertainment up another notch. I reached into my pocket and pulled out one of the fire crackers that were just sitting there. A classmate quickly came to my aid with a box of matches, lit the cracker, and away it went towards the entrance of the classroom. To my shock and chagrin, the vice-principal of the school walked right through the doorway into the path of the flying missile, which exploded with a big bang, meters away from his face. My life, I thought, was suddenly over.

"Who did it?" he queried, as a once tumultuous classroom became silent with fear and trepidation flooding my soul. After a short period of resistance from my die-hard supporters who refused to "give me up," a hand could be seen rising into the air, as Ted nervously pointed me out with words of betrayal: "He did it, Sir!" With this revelation, I was commanded to go to the principal's office, where I was later chided for my less than desirable behavior and told to go home and never to return. In other words, I was expelled. That was the Floyd that Travis knew.

That afternoon when I got home and nervously broke the news to my mother, she became livid. Her son had done it again. He was sent home from school for the fourth time due to his distasteful and undisciplined behavior in the classroom. The next morning, she woke me up very early, ordered me to get dressed, and then marched me back onto the school compound and into the lobby of the principal's office. Upon arrival, she demanded from the secretary an audience with the principal. To my surprise, the principal entertained her conversation about giving me another chance for the fourth time. With tears in her eyes, she unyieldingly pleaded with him to give me one last chance. After much thought, the principal relented and warned me, "This is your last chance; you had better make good use of this opportunity and be glad you have a mother like this!" With that said, I was back in school again, only this time I had a different attitude.

That day in the principal's office signaled the turning point in my life and set the stage for what was to be a great future for me. While my mother was pleading on my behalf, it became convincingly clear how much she believed in me, even when I did not believe in myself. Along with the principal, they both believed in me, which consequently triggered my belief in myself. They saw greatness within me and I decided to unlock it. I went on to become a mentor to other students, improved dramatically in my academic performance, and graduated from high school to the delight of my parents. Since graduating from high school, I have received a Bachelor of Arts degree, a Masters degree, a Doctoral degree, and many other professional certifications. Professionally, I have served as a minister, military officer (Capt. Ret.) in the Canadian Armed Forces, psychotherapist, consultant, motivational speaker, life strategist, and business coach. This was the Floyd that Travis had just met to his astonishment.

Having gotten a vision of who I could become, I chose to believe in myself and pursue my dream, and I decided to live the best life possible. I now live by the mantra, "There's Greatness Within You" and believe that regardless of who you are or where you're from, you also have greatness within. It is my belief that where you are now is not where you are always going to be. In other words, you are more than you currently are, and it may just be the time for you to exceed yourself. Exceed Yourself, therefore, seeks to provide you with insights and strategies in unleashing your potential so that you may become your best self possible.

This book was written for people whose desire is to be the best in what they do, whether in their personal and/or professional life. If you apply these principles in your daily life, you will experience a paradigm shift in your mindset, enabling you to take empowered actions that will transform your life, career, and bank account.

In the pages ahead we will explore, how the conscious and subconscious domains of the mind impact our life and success. We will also identify effective ways to train our minds so that we may take empowered actions that will take us far beyond what we have ever thought possible. The bottom line is this: "There's Greatness Within You" and it's time for you to unlock it, exceed yourself, and live your best life possible! Please note that some of the names of real individuals have been disguised to protect their confidentiality or privacy. WARNING: Reading this book may change your life!

PART ONE

THERE'S GREATNESS WITHIN YOU

Chapter 1

THE POWER OF HUNGER

*"Wanting something is not good enough.
You must hunger for it" ~ Les Brown*

The one thing most successful people have in common is hunger. The power of hunger will set you apart from the competition and take you to the next level of your life, career, and business. In fact, successful people win because they have a strong desire to succeed, whether it's in sports, business, or any career path they pursue. If you are going to be successful and continue to be successful in life, you need to understand the hunger factor and its impact on your success; you need to get hungry and you need to stay hungry.

THE "HUNGER" FACTOR

A lot of people give up too easily, throw in the towel too quickly, and retire themselves to the sideline of life too early. But why? It all comes down to a lack of hunger. Take Henry Ford for instance. Despite his setbacks in his early life, he still managed to achieve massive success.[1] Born on July 30, 1863, Ford grew up on his family's farm in Wayne County, Michigan. When Ford was 13 years old, he received a pocket watch as a gift from his father, which he eagerly took apart and promptly reassembled perfectly. This got the attention of some of his friends and neighbors who requested that he fixed their timepieces also.

With an appetite to fix things, Ford left his farm home with big aspirations at the age of 16 to take up an apprenticeship as a mechanist in Detroit, Michigan. Despite his enthusiasm as an engineer, Ford experienced failure. He spent all the money he received from his first investors without producing a car. Just as the investment from his financial backers was short-lived, even so was his first company: The Detroit Automotive Company. It went bankrupt. Regardless of Ford's failures, he refused to give up. He was hungry and would not give up. He eventually succeeded, becoming one of America's most successful businessmen and a pioneer in the automobile industry. According to Ford, "failure is simply the opportunity to begin again, this time more intelligently."[2]

Like Henry Ford, we can all realize our dreams if we are hungry. For the record, hunger is a strong desire or craving for something. It is a fervent desire to achieve your goals, dreams, or aspirations. So how badly do you want it? How badly do you want to be that elite athlete? How badly do you want that sculpted physique? How badly do you want to succeed in your field or industry? If you truly want to achieve the success you have been dreaming about, you have to be hungry. You need to have an "I must" attitude. You have to be like the general who burned the boats upon arriving on the shore, leaving him with only one option. As Jim Collins put it, "Succeed or die."[3]

In my experience as a life and business coach, I have noticed that no obstacle is big enough to stand in the path of an individual who is hungry for a particular goal. He or she will make the necessary sacrifice. He or she will work hard, stay focused, and develop the skills required to move to the next level. In other words, unless you desire to achieve your dream like you desire oxygen, you won't succeed. This is what makes the difference between those who thrive and those who just exist; those who are good and those who are great.

GET HUNGRY

After three suspensions, one expulsion and a mother pleading with my high school principal to give me a fourth chance, I finally got it. I started an inventory of my life by asking myself some tough questions. Questions such as "What's wrong with you?" "When are you going to stop hurting your parents?" The life changing question though, was this: "What are you going to do with this new opportunity?" I could hear the chattering in my head as I followed up with a second and third question. "What do you want to do with the rest of your life and who do you want to become?" It didn't take me long to make the decision. I decided; I am going to be better! I got hungry! I decided to become more.

Even though I didn't know exactly what I wanted at the time, I knew exactly what I didn't want. I didn't want to continue being a failure. I didn't want to continue being average. I didn't want to continue being poor. I didn't want to be taken advantage of like my parents, who were preyed upon by unscrupulous people because of their inability to read and write. This dialogue with myself created for me a mind-shift and a desire for something better—a drive to design my future. Suffice it to say, this drive has led me on an exciting journey of self-discovery—a journey that has helped me identify my purpose and has given me a life now lived with meaning and tremendous success. My desire for something better changed my life and it will change yours, too.

How might getting hungry change your life? In most circles, hunger is defined as a strong desire or craving. It is a drive to pursue persistently what you feel called to do. This craving is usually precipitated by a search for meaning and purpose—a pre-requisite for all those who aspire to unlock their greatness. It wasn't until I started searching for meaning and purpose that I developed hunger. Furthermore, as my purpose became clearer, my hunger intensified. Thus, finding your purpose helps to create hunger, which will, in turn, propel you towards being your best self. Here is the deal! If you haven't yet found your purpose, your first duty is to find out what it is, because until you find it, you will not experience greatness and fulfillment in life. You will continue to be average, with average results in what you do. It is my belief that each of us has a purpose, something we are "called to do." I consider my purpose as that of helping others find theirs and live the best life possible! What's yours?

Have you found your purpose? Do you know what it is? What are you passionate about? What gets you excited? Finding your purpose helps to fuel hunger which will, in turn, propel you towards optimum performance and an extraordinary life. We are not just talking about a job here. We are talking about a calling—something that brings you joy and fulfillment no matter how challenging doing it is. It is what gets you out of bed early in the morning and keeps you up late at night with excitement. As Dr. Dennis Kimbro put it, "A career is what you pay for; a calling is what you're made for."[4]

When asked by an attendee at a conference in 2007 for the most valuable piece of advice he would give on becoming successful, Steve Jobs remarked; "You have to have a lot of passion for what you do… because if you don't, any rational person will give up." In other words, if you don't love what you do, sooner or later you are going to give up. You are going to fail. But if you have passion—a hunger for what you do, you will persevere, no matter what, and will ultimately succeed.

STAY HUNGRY

It is quite easy to get distracted in life when your purpose is not clear. Once you are locked into your purpose however, success is more achievable. This is because living purposefully keeps you hungry. So here's the deal! Stay hungry by keeping the "why" for doing what you are doing present every day. As holocaust survivor Fredrick Nietzche put it, "He who has a why to live for can bear with almost any how."[6]

Those who have a "why" to live for, are unstoppable! They are purposeful and internally driven. They are hungry! They keep believing in themselves and in their dreams even if no one else believes in them. They don't just "kind of want success"; their life depends on it. For them, failure is not an option; success is their only path.

So how do you stay hungry? By simply deciding on the "why" behind the goal or dream, you are pursuing. Your "why" is what intrinsically motivates you. It is that force within that drives you. Why you want something is, therefore, more important than what you want and how you get what you want. The "how" and "what" may change, but the "why" will not because it is a part of who you are, a part of your destiny.

For a fact, when you think about why you want to do something, the actions you take will be more intentional and the results astounding. Simon Sinek correctly conceptualizes this in his book *Start with Why* by asserting that knowing your why is more important than knowing your "what" and your "how."[7] While most people start with "what" and then proceed to "how," successful people start with "why."

Once you become driven by your "why," no obstacle will be too big to stop you. No sacrifice is too hard to make and no price too high to pay as you pursue your dream. This is why I concur with Berton Braley who once said the following:

> "If you want a thing bad enough
> To go out and fight for it,
> Work day and night for it,
> Give up your time, your peace and your sleep for it
> If life seems all empty and useless without it
> And all that you scheme and you dream is about it,
>
> If you'll simply go after that thing that you want
> With all your capacity,
> Strength, and sagacity,
> Faith, hope, and confidence, stern pertinacity,
>
> If neither cold poverty, famished and gaunt,
> Nor sickness nor pain
> Of body and brain
> Can turn you away from the thing that you want,
>
> If dogged and grim you besiege and beset it,
> You'll get it."[8]

Hunger is, therefore, a very powerful characteristic of the successful life. Likewise, if you are going to be successful in your life or line of work, you have to experience the hunger factor. Get hungry and stay hungry. That's how winning is done!

Chapter 2

THE PSYCHOLOGY OF SUCCESS

"Life consists of what a man is thinking of all day"
~ Ralph Waldo Emerson

I heard voices, voices that kept interrupting me, telling me what I couldn't do each time I tried to pursue my dream! My breakthrough came, however, after I stepped back from myself and confronted the self-defeating thoughts that kept running around in my head. The human brain is often compared to a computer with its fascinating operating system. This operating system, which is the software that supports the computer's basic function, is comprised of a set of instructions that tell it what to do.

Human beings have operating systems and the brain uses instructions, too. Those instructions are like software—pieces of information that include our beliefs, values, and views of ourselves and the world. Our behavior is, therefore, a reflection of our thinking. So what's happening in there, in that brain of yours? Could it be that we are the composite of what we think about, and is it possible that believing in ourselves has the potential of taking our lives to a whole new level?

MEET THE TWO SELVES

A thought is a conversation with yourself.[9] You have them every day, but why? When I considered writing this book, I had a conversation with myself as to whether or not it was the right thing to do. "It's too time consuming!" I said to myself. "The book won't sell!" I chided. "Why spend all that time writing, when you could be dedicating your time and effort to something less tedious?" I counseled. Here is an important question as we seek to unravel this internal exchange.

Who is talking to whom? According to W. Timothy Gallwey in his book *The Inner Game of Tennis*, the "I" and the "myself" are two separate entities. If there weren't two entities, then there would not have been a conversation in the first place. The "I" seems to be the one always giving instructions, while the "myself" is the one taking the advice and performing the action.[10] In other words, there is a constant dialogue taking place in our heads whenever we attempt to make a decision or take an action.

The type of relationship that exists between "I" and "myself" significantly impacts the actions to be taken. Based on the relationship, the action can be effective or ineffective, negative or positive. In other words, the key to getting better results is to improve the relationship between the conscious mind—the "I"—and the subconscious mind—the "myself."

I remember when I decided to go to college. It was mentally frustrating. I kept stepping into my own way by listening to the negative instructions I was giving to myself. It wasn't until I stopped telling myself what I couldn't do and started telling myself what I could do that I was finally able to get focused on pursuing my dream and ultimately graduated from college with a Bachelors degree.

The key to getting peace and harmony between these two entities is to quiet the mind through reflection and contemplation. This means "less calculating, judging, worrying, fearing, hoping, trying, regretting, controlling, jittering or distracting."[11] Instead, just see things as they are. This non-judgmental awareness is simply resisting the temptation to add or subtract from the facts. It is being at peace with oneself by freeing the mind of criticism and creating congruence between thoughts and actions.

Suffice it to say, our inner conversations are driven by our internal conditioning and the programming we received from our environment as children growing up. Your view of the world is, therefore, a reflection of the view you hold of yourself, a view that is rooted in the subconscious mind, the place that influences most of the things we say and do.

THE MIND IS LIKE AN ICEBERG

The mind is like an iceberg! This metaphor, once used by psychologist Sigmund Freud to describe the minds capacity, is an apt way to shine light on how the subconscious mind influences human behavior. As is depicted in the diagram below, the portion that is visible to the eyes is just a small fraction—10%—compared to the rest of the iceberg—90%—that lies beneath the ocean's surface. Similarly, the mind, which is the intangible portion of the brain, consists of both the conscious and the subconscious mind.

It is popularly believed that 10% of the mind's capacity

is the conscious mind, while the remaining 90% is the subconscious. There are others, however, who believe that it is more a 5–95 % ratio.[12] Regardless of the ratio, it is important to understand that the subconscious mind has a significant influence on your behavior. The conscious mind which accounts for at least 10% of the mind's capacity is, therefore, where our conscious control of willpower, analysis, and decision making reside. On the other hand, the subconscious mind accounts for about 90% of the mind's capacity. This is where most of our influence comes from as it relates to our behavior. In other words the subconscious mind wields the major influence over what we do, and we are to a large extent on auto-pilot when it comes to our beliefs, values, identity, self-confidence, and habits.

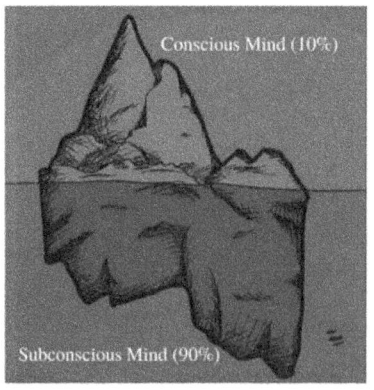

Conscious Control Of:
- Willpower
- Analysis
- Decision

Automated Regarding:
- Beliefs
- Values
- Habits
- Self-confidence

Think of the last time you drove or walked home from work. By following my command to think, you just engaged the conscious mind through the process of memory recall. The process of walking down the street to your house without consciously needing to be alert to your surroundings is the work of the subconscious mind. But how was this made possible? According to Shad Helmstetter in his book *What to Say When You Talk To Yourself*, this automated behavior is due to the fact that the subconscious mind has been programmed over-time to engage in this particular behavior without your having to think about it.[13] To put it another way, your subconscious conditioning determines your belief; your belief determines your actions; your actions determine your outcome.

Your Conditioning ▸ Your Belief ▸ Your Actions ▸ Your Outcome

While the conscious mind is the creative mind, "the subconscious mind is primarily a repository of stimulus-response tapes, derived from instincts and learned experiences."[14] It is important to your success and well-being, therefore, to become aware of your subconscious conditioning and how this has been impacting your actions and outcomes in life. Once this is done, a shift in your mindset towards more positive, empowering thoughts will be required in order to replace the energy-draining and self-defeating beliefs that are destined to sabotage your success.

We can conclude, therefore, that the subconscious mind is more powerful than the conscious mind. This means, that your subconscious mind is in the driver's seat of your life, more than 90% of the time. Since the conscious mind is what we use to visualize the future, assess the past, and decide what decisions to make as we solve problems, getting the programs in the subconscious mind aligned with the conscious is a necessity if you are to live a successful life.

PROGRAMMING THE MIND TO WIN

We have all been programmed. At some point in our lives, we have downloaded from our parents, the environment, our teachers, religious leaders, and our culture beliefs that either set us up to succeed or set us up to fail. In fact, the biggest obstacle to our success is the limitations programmed into our subconscious mind. Consequently, how we live our lives on a daily basis is rooted in the beliefs that we have developed over the years from the people or situations that programmed us. This means that the actions and behavior of a person's life are a true reflection of their inner belief. As

James Allen asserted, "All that a man achieves and all that he fails to achieve is the direct result of his own thoughts." [15] Since your belief drives your behavior, it is important to change your belief if you are to get the results you ultimately want.

According to Tony Robbins; "all personal breakthroughs begin with a change in beliefs." A change in your psychology is, therefore, necessary in order for you to take the breakthrough actions required to win in your personal and professional life. In other words, just as how you were set up to fail by some of your previous programming, you can set yourself up for success by programming yourself to succeed. Here is how you do it!

Take the Pain Versus Pleasure Approach

One of the best ways in programming your mind to win is by using the "pain versus pleasure" approach to change your belief system. First, "get your brain to associate massive pain to the old belief. You must feel deep in your gut that not only has this belief cost you pain in the past, but it's costing you in the present and, ultimately, can only bring you pain in the future."[17] Second, associate pleasure with the idea of pursuing and achieving the thing for which you desire. Think about the joy of having a satisfying relationship, a successful business, finishing college, or whatever it is that you want to accomplish. By so doing, you are conditioning your mind to override your self-defeating programming as you set yourself up to win.

As human beings, we generally have an aversion to things that cause us pain, and an affinity to things that bring us pleasure. By taking a "pain versus pleasure" approach to life, we are retraining our belief system to focus less on the temporary pain and more on the long-term desire to achieve success, which is associated with tremendous pleasure.

Practice Positive Self-talk

While the conscious mind may say, "I want success," if the subconscious mind says no, you may end up not getting what you asked for. Suffice it to say, we are not victims of our subconscious programming. This is because the conscious mind can step in, stop a behavior, and create a new one while preprogrammed behavior is taking place. It should be noted, however, that the subconscious programming will take over the very moment when your conscious mind is not paying attention.[18] This is why an alignment between the subconscious mind and your goals is required if there is going to be follow-through after a command is given by the conscious mind. One of the best ways to create such an alignment is through positive self-talk.

Positive self-talk can be defined as the process of overriding "our past negative programming by erasing or replacing it with conscious, positive new directions."[19] The use of self-talk, has a way of boosting self-confidence and, when utilized correctly, enables an individual to perform at his/her very best. One of the most powerful approaches I have used in therapy and coaching to deal with limiting beliefs is to identify the source of these self-defeating beliefs and then work with the individuals to override them intentionally. Here is an example: Let's say you have been having thoughts about being a failure whenever you think about pursuing a career or your dream of starting your own business. As you assess this way of thinking, you notice that, as a child, you were made to feel like a failure when you did not meet the expectations of the people around you. Having identified the source of these messages that you have been telling yourself, the next step would be to counteract them intentionally with positive truths in your life. This could mean telling yourself, (using your first-name,) "John, if you have been successful before, you can be successful again."

The secret to taking your life to the next level is, therefore, to quiet those negative self-talk you have been having with yourself and replace them with more positive ones. Interestingly enough, research have shown that positive self-talk is "one of the most effective, least-utilized tools available to master the psyche and foster life success."[20] With that said, begin to program your mind with the information that will impact your desired behavior and outcome. You can do this by using more empowering words on a daily basis, by choosing what you watch on TV, the books you read, the music you listen to, the people you spend time with, and the things you tell yourself. Since you are constantly being programmed, make sure no one else is programming you but you yourself.

Chapter 3

UNLOCK YOUR GREATNESS

"Never underestimate the power of dreams and the influence of the human spirit. We are all the same in this notion: The potential for greatness lives within each of us."
~ Wilma Rudolph

I remember it as if it were yesterday! It was a bright and sunny Sunday morning. As I enthusiastically raked the leaves in the front yard, Mama walked over to me and remarked, "You are going to be great!" I was stunned! How could this 11-year-old boy from such a humble beginning and with such poor grades in elementary school achieve such a lofty feat of being great? Looking back now, I have to admit that my success had a lot to do with those six words spoken to me by Mama at a time when I didn't even understand what greatness meant.

We are all born with the potential for greatness! Though no one is born great, we all enter this world with the seed of greatness that was sown by the Creator. In spite of this fact, however, only a handful of people are able to unleash their potential and rise to the height of the extraordinary. Here's why! Greatness doesn't show up by osmosis; you have to be intentional about it. Greatness, therefore, is grown, not born, and can be unlocked by upgrading your self-image and by believing in yourself.

GREATNESS IS GROWN

The mighty oak towers majestically over its counterpart in the field. This gigantic tree did not become great overnight. It had its beginning in a small, slightly rounded, brown object called an acorn. Within this acorn lies the latent potential to become an oak tree. Once it is put into a nurturing environment, its innate power wakes up and starts the process of becoming an oak tree. Like an acorn that unlocks its greatness and grows into a mighty oak tree, we all can become great. The Greek philosopher Epictetus asserted, "We all carry the seeds of greatness within us, but we need an image as a point of focus in order that they may sprout."[21]

My sprouting moment came during a conversation with a co-worker of mine while taking a break from serving tables as a bar attendant years ago. As I leaned against the bar counter in the hotel dining room on this particular afternoon, my co-worker asked me a life-changing question: "What are you doing here?" Dennis had known me for over two years and felt that I was living far below my potential.

As a high school graduate, I had completed the pre-requisites to pursue higher education; I also had the qualification for a better paying job, but here I was working for "peanuts." Dennis' question again ignited the greatness within me. It triggered introspection and caused me to revisit the desire I had during the experience with my mother and my high school principal in his office years before. My desire to be better had been capped, but this question immediately shifted my mindset and blew the lid off my potential. With an inventory of where I was in life, where I wanted to be, and the possible ways of getting there, the possibilities now appeared limitless.

That was the last day I worked at that job and it was one of the best decisions I have ever made in my life. That day, I became rich, though I was poor, because I now had a dream. I was going to improve myself, pursue higher education, and help people to live life to the fullest. Suffice it to say, I have grown from an acorn into an oak and I am still growing.

Journalist and New York Times bestselling author Daniel Coyle asserted in his book, *The Talent Code*, "Greatness is not born. It is grown." Coyle suggested that what differentiates the good from the great is the ability to operate purposefully at the edges of one's ability.[22] Growing greatness is not dependent on genes or pedigree; it's about exceeding yourself. It's about choosing a goal "just beyond your present abilities"[23] and pursuing it through deep practice, ignition, and masterful coaching.[24]

Deep Practice

Deep practice means engaging in an activity repeatedly while being attentive, hungry, focused, and even desperate. The rule is first to "chunk it up." This means taking the task and dividing it into small chunks, rather than approaching it as a whole.

The second thing to do is to "repeat it." Repeating it simply means building your skills or competence by taking action and by repeating the action daily until you experience mastery. Research shows that the world's renowned experts practice anywhere between three and five hours per day regardless of the skills they pursue.[25]

The third rule in the three rules of deep practice is to "learn to feel it." It is about the feeling evoked "while reaching, falling short and reaching again."[26] This usually occurs in a cyclical manner until the goal is achieved. The idea here is that in order to get good at something, you have to be prepared to be bad at it first.

People who engage in deep practice fail fast and accelerate their level of success at a faster pace. It is an approach that can be summarized in the words of Samuel Becket: "Try again. Fail again. Fail better."[27]

Ignition

While deep practice is crucial in developing your skills, this cannot be done without passion, motivation, and the will to succeed. Though motivation at times can come from within, most of the time, it comes from without. A powerful way to ignite the power within and get your motivation fired up, therefore, is simply to tell yourself, "If he/she can do that, I can do it, too."

As was mentioned earlier in this chapter, one has to be hungry and motivated. In the book The Talent Code, Daniel Coyle called this "ignition." He asserted, "Ignition and deep practice work together to produce skill in exactly the same way that a gas tank combines with an engine to produce velocity in an automobile."[28] In other words, ignition acts as the source of energy, while deep practice utilizes the energy to move you forward on a path of massive success.[29]

Masterful Coaching

Masterful coaching is like farming. It is a careful and deliberate cultivation of a person's potential. It is helping individuals to become the best that they can possibly be. The word *coach* is derived from the "horse-drawn coaches that were developed in the town of Kocs during the fifteenth century." [30] While the coach was originally developed as a vehicle to carry royalty, it was later used to transport mail and valuables. Suffice it to say, a coach is "something or someone, who carries a valued person from where they are to where they want to be."[31]

For those who are going to step into their greatness and live life to the fullest; coaching is a necessity. Quite frankly, it's not possible to maximize your potential in any area of your life without the assistance of a coach, mentor, or someone who is referred to in martial arts as a master. Masterful coaching, which is personal training for the mind, will take your life to the next level and create for you a highly rewarding life that is full of satisfaction, fulfillment, and success.

UPDATING YOUR SELF-IMAGE FOR SUCCESS

I was quite young when I first heard the biblical phrase,

"As a man thinks in his heart so is he." I really did not get it until during my early adult years when I started on a journey of self-discovery through daily meditation and quiet reflection. I finally got it! We perceive the world based on how we view ourselves! This was my experience as the thoughts I had about myself got in the way of my progress. In other words, I did not have a healthy concept of myself, and it was sabotaging my success. To my surprise, once I changed my view of myself, I noticed that my life picked up momentum, and I started noticing limitless possibilities.

Today, the findings are compelling! Indeed, you are what you think about. According to Nathaniel Branden, a psychiatrist and self-esteem expert, "no other factor is more important in people's psychological development and motivation than the value judgments they make about themselves."[32] If you are going to step into your greatness and exceed yourself, updating your self-image is, therefore, going to be a must. To do this you need to understand the basics of self-image; you need to confront the enemy within; and last, but not least, you need to develop a plan to build your self-image.

Understanding the Self-image

A friend once told me he didn't feel good enough. In his own words, he didn't think he was attractive. "My ears are too big and even family members have ridiculed me about them from the time I was a child." This view of himself became internalized to the point where he started seeing himself as not good enough. The view he had about himself is referred to as *self-image*, while the feelings he had about himself is referred to as *self-esteem*. Both the view and the feelings he had about himself could have had a tremendous impact on his *self-confidence*—how secure he felt within himself and his abilities.

Consciously or unconsciously, "each of us carries about with us, a mental blue print or picture of ourselves."[33] The picture we hold of ourselves can make a big difference between success and failure, be it in our personal or professional lives. This view is our own construct of who we think we are. It is a reflection of our beliefs which we have subconsciously built and accepted as our truth. Surprisingly enough, these beliefs have been formed through the interactions we have had in the past with our successes, failures, friends, relatives, and the community, especially during our early childhood years.

Suffice it to say, once you incorporate a belief about yourself within this picture, it becomes your truth and informs the way you live and interact with the rest of the world. This means that your actions, feelings, behavior, and abilities will become consistent with the views you hold about yourself. As Zig Ziglar often says in his motivational talks, "It's impossible to consistently behave in a manner inconsistent with how we see ourselves. We can do very few things in a positive way if we feel negative about ourselves." In other words, "you will 'act like' the sort of person you conceive yourself to be."[34]

The Enemy Within

We can be our worst enemy. As the African proverb suggests, "When there is no enemy within, the enemy outside cannot hurt you." The view we have of ourselves does have a significant impact on our relationships, our personal, and our professional lives. In fact, the main reason many people fail to grow and reach their full potential is due to low self-esteem.[35] People who hold themselves in high esteem are generally more confident and exude outward signs of an inward radiance. On the contrary, people with low self-esteem and low self-image present themselves to the world as afraid and timid and tend to sabotage their success by getting in their own way. Internally, there resides an enemy—the critical and negative self.

It is virtually impossible for you to do anything without being affected by your concept of self. That means that your level of success in life will be tied intrinsically to the beliefs you have about yourself and the negative or positive image you have stored in your mind. Since self-esteem creates such a huge impact on how you interact with the rest of the world, it is important to become aware of your daily mental chattering.

If you find yourself evaluating your self-worth by comparing yourself with others, there may be an enemy within. It is not very easy to "keep up with the Kardashians." To look like, act like, and live like everybody else while pursuing your dream is a hindrance to progress. Embracing who you are is liberating and will make you more creative, more inventive, and more progressive. Another thing that indicates there is an enemy within is living someone else's dream or living out someone else's script. It's important to live your own truth and pursue your own dream. It may be wise to ask yourself on a regular basis, "Whose life am I living? Is it mine or is it someone else's?" As Brene Brown so powerfully advised in the sub-heading of her book *The Gifts of Imperfection*, "Let go of who you think you're supposed to be and embrace who you are."[36]

Building Your Self-image

One's self-image can be changed. The first step, however, is to acknowledge that you have a self-image or self-esteem problem. Bear in mind that awareness is the pre-requisite of change. Since you cannot change what you are not aware of, it is important to take an inventory of the inner-self first. This will help you to identify the areas of your self-image that you need to change. With that said, try the following additional tips to build your self-image:

- Make a list of your strengths and assets and remind yourself of them each day.
- Think of qualities that others compliment you on and accept them even if you do not believe them completely.
- Stop comparing yourself with others. This is an act of futility, as there will always be someone else who is in a better position than you are. If you have to compare yourself with anyone, it should be you, as you strive to be better today than you were yesterday.
- Quiet the negative mental chattering by telling yourself to shut up or by thinking of contradictions to these thoughts.
- Accept your imperfections. This means accepting your mistakes and the things about yourself you cannot change.
- Celebrate your achievements. It is good for your mental state and serves as a reminder of your abilities, build resilience, and inoculates you against the bad.

Where you are now is definitely not where you have to remain. You can change. Building a healthy self-image is, therefore, of paramount importance for your success since "all your actions, feelings, behavior – even your abilities – are always consistent with this self-image."[37]

Believe in Yourself

Believing in oneself has its payoff. I believe that, as human beings, we are all born with the seed of greatness. We all have the same 24 hours in each day, yet some of us succeed and others don't. You may be thinking. "Oh, right. Some people are born into privilege and so they are destined for success." You may be right, but the majority of the people who succeed do so because they made it happen. Then why is it that so few people succeed, and so many fail? I have concluded that one of the main reasons is the lack of belief in oneself.

If you are to grow and become all that you are potentially capable of becoming, you are going to have to start believing in yourself. This means having confidence in your abilities and placing a high value on who you are and who you are capable of becoming. We cannot expect others to value us more than we value ourselves. Hence, if you put a low value on yourself, don't expect someone else to raise the price. Interestingly enough, leveraging the power of self-belief will make a huge difference in your life and provide you with the results you desire. Here's how self-belief works.

1. Self-belief Makes You More Optimistic

There was once an elephant at a circus that was chained to a pole as an infant. He tried to break away, but was not strong enough to do so. Over time, he became monstrous. One day, the circus accidentally went on fire and the elephant died. He was enormous and could have easily ripped the pole out of the ground and run away to safety, but there was a self-limiting belief in his mind that told him he would not be able to do it, and so he didn't try. Indeed, your ability to succeed is all in the mind.

Since we perceive the world base on how we view ourselves, a person who believes in him- or herself tends to be more confident and sees the world through a lens of optimism. In essence, an optimist is not chained to past failures or current challenges, but instead, uses them as inspiration and holds his/her head high in anticipation of a better future. Winston Churchill said poignantly, that "the optimist sees opportunity in every danger; the pessimist sees danger in every opportunity."[38] If you are to succeed in any field, therefore, you have to look for the opportunity in every adversity.

2. Self-belief Stimulates Action

A lot of people who set goals end up not following through on taking the appropriate action. In my experience as a professional coach, I have discovered that one of the reasons so many people do not follow through is because they approach their goals from a place of timidity and disbelief. This belief becomes a self-fulfilling prophecy as they become choked on their self-doubt, abandoning the plans they had for the realization of their goals.

On the contrary, self-belief stimulates action, creates clarity of thought and opens the mind to ask empowering questions as you pursue your goals. In essence, you will be able to explore different possibilities and come up with more creative solutions to deal with the task at hand.

3. Self-belief Attracts Success

Here is what I have learned over the years about success. It is more about what we attract and less about what we pursue. In other words, success is something you attract as a result of the person you have become. Suffice it to say, if you emit disbelieving vibes, others will pick up on it and the same energy you send out will return to you. If you approach life believing in yourself, you will be more positive and more optimistic, which will likely attract others to you and ultimately, to the help or resources you need to achieve success.

Here are four habits you can practice as you strive to develop your self-belief.

Habit 1: Acknowledge and Celebrate Your Accomplishments

Recall and savor the feelings of your accomplishments. Commend yourself for what a great job you did. Celebrate your accomplishment with family and friends. If you want to go a step further, reward yourself with a bath, a massage, or some other pleasurable activity that you would like to indulge in. This will help to incorporate success into your self-image, making you eventually view yourself as someone of more value.

These moments of celebration, incidentally, are a pause to notice the good things in our lives, as well as a reminder of the skills, talents, and abilities we possess.[39] Celebrating your accomplishments and recalling times when you were successful, therefore, can definitely boost your concept of self.

Habit 2: Pay Attention to Your Self-talk

Be careful what you say to yourself; a person's worse enemy is him or herself. Pay attention to your internal dialogue; it can set you up to fail. You have to be careful about what you say to yourself because you are always listening. If you have to talk to yourself, make sure it is positive and empowering. If you find yourself having negative mental chattering, interrupt them immediately. "Replace them—drown them out—with positive self-talk and images."[40]

Habit 3: Have an "I Can Do It Too" Attitude

Before Roger Bannister ran a mile in less than four minutes, no one else had ever done it. In the weeks following Banisters' phenomenal accomplishment, Australian John Landy also rose to the occasion and broke the four-minute barrier. Within the next three years, other athletes started breaking it in droves. What was it that led to these other athletes' breaking the four-minute barrier in such a short period of time? It was simply this: They had an "I can do it, too" attitude! These athletes "had received a clear signal—*you can do this too*—and the four minute mark, once an insurmountable wall, was instantly recast as a stepping-stone." [41] Like the many others who have done what you are attempting to do, tell yourself, "If others have done it, I can do it, too."

Habit 4: Grow Yourself

I have to agree with motivational speaker Jim Rohn, who once said, "If you want to have more, you have to become more." Self-belief is truly a reflection of how you feel about your skills and abilities in relation to how you handle your various tasks in life. That being said, the more you grow as an individual, the more your skills, abilities, and capacity will improve. The more you improve, the more you will believe in yourself. As a matter of fact, learning will have to be a lifelong process if you are to better yourself and be successful at what you do. Growing yourself is, therefore, not an option.

So, are you ready for greatness? Most of us, desire more! We want to experience success of some sort. It may be to attend college or university, to get married, to get out of poverty, or just to push ourselves to the edge of our limits. This desire to pursue and realize your dream is possible. You must, however, develop a sense of hunger as you pursue your dream, condition your mind to win, and be intentional about unlocking your greatness through personal growth and by never losing sight of your "why."

Reflection

WHAT? (WHAT SPOKE TO YOU)

_____
_____
_____
_____
_____
_____
_____
_____

SO WHAT? (YOUR TAKE-AWAY)

_____
_____
_____
_____
_____
_____
_____
_____

NOW WHAT? (YOUR PLAN OF ACTION)

_____
_____
_____
_____
_____
_____
_____
_____

Part Two

IT'S POSSIBLE

Chapter 4

TUNE INTO YOUR PURPOSE

"The two most important days in your life are the day you are born and the day you find out why." ~ Mark Twain

One of the central, existential questions to ask oneself is "why am I here?" Once we can live the answer to this question, our lives will be lived with more meaning and fulfillment. By "why," I mean purpose. Though finding your purpose can be a challenge, it is an essential step in figuring out your next move. Purpose provides us with a reason to exist and an objective to pursue. It is, in essence, the driving force behind a successful life. So get clear on your purpose, understand that purpose has its payoffs, and continue to build your competence.

GET CLEAR

Academy award winner Sidney Poitier was born in Miami during a visit by his Bahamian parents who traveled there to sell tomatoes. Poitier grew up in the Bahamas until he was 15 years old. At the age of 15, he was sent to live with his brother in Miami, but moved to New York at the age of 17. He later joined the American Negro Theatre there, but was rejected by audiences because of his thick Bahamian accent. Poitier spent the next six months learning American English and at the end of the six months, auditioned again and was accepted. Today, he is known as one of the best actors in history, as well as the first black actor to win an Academy Award for best actor. Sidney Poitier was clear on his purpose and would not relent, regardless of the setbacks he encountered.

Like Poitier, tuning into your purpose requires that you are clear about your "why." Your why is that irresistible thing in your life that drives what you do and can be found where your passion and skills intersect. It is what keeps you up at night, gets you out of bed in the morning, and fires you up for the day. People who are clear about their purpose are fueled from the inside out. With this kind of motivation they usually get the job done. This is what drives success.

The anticipation was building. The desire to conquer the air was high. Samuel Pierpont Langley, one of the most esteemed scientists in the United States, set out on a quest in the early 1900s to build a person-carrying-machine. Langley's stature as secretary of the Smithsonian Institute gave him great credibility, and he was the only flight experimenter to receive government funding for such a project. The Department of Defense (then War Department) contributed $50,000 towards the development of Langley's flying machine. The Smithsonian chipped in with a similar amount, and Langley's friends, including some of the most powerful men in business and government, lent their support in order to make Langley's dream of being the first man to fly an airplane a reality. Langley seemed to have all the support, education, and money required to pull off the job. On October 7, 1903, Langley attempted flight, but was not successful. On December 8, he tried again, but again failed.[42]

Just nine days later, Wilbur and Orville Wright became the first to fly an airplane, and a small group of people witnessed this unforgettable breakthrough in aviation history.[43] The brothers had no government funding, no business or government connections, and when the launch took place, there was no fanfare. What caused Langley, who had all the trappings of success, to fail, and the Wright brothers, who had none of that, to succeed? Though they both had the same goal, the Wright brothers, unlike Langley, were tuned in to their purpose. Their purpose was clear and they were driven and motivated to accomplish their goal in spite of four years of experimenting with trial and errors.

The truth is that having what Napoleon Hill called "definiteness of purpose"[44] and consistency beat talent every time. Knowing your purpose, therefore, makes it easier to decide on the actions to be taken and helps you funnel your time, energy, and effort in the right direction.

PURPOSE HAS PAYOFFS

Growing up was difficult. In my parents' two bedroom house tucked away in the rural hills of eastern Jamaica, we lacked running water. There was no plumbing in the house and we had to bathe and cook in a make-shift bathroom and kitchen, respectively, outside the house. Shoes were luxury items and were worn only to school and to church in order to lengthen their days. Papa was a small farmer who worked very hard, night and day, but still didn't have enough to pay the bills at the end of the week. Mama on the other hand, was a homemaker, whose role was to nurture the eight kids and, at the same time, juggle the little money Papa brought home. At times, she would invest some of the funds selling baked goods to the more fortunate in the neighborhood. With the return on her investment, she was able to pay some of the weekly bills and put a little more food on the table.

As I assessed the daily struggle that my parents went through, I decided that I was going to grow myself educationally and get out of poverty, even if I had to die trying. This liberating thought has since been my greatest motivation and keeps propelling me every day towards my destiny. From my experience, I have to conclude that being driven by purpose pays high dividends.

Before you take the next action, it may be prudent for you first to find a worthy purpose. There can be no true success without a purpose-driven life. One of the best definitions of success that I have ever heard comes from Earl Nightingale who once said, "Success is the progressive realization of a worthy ideal."[45] Put another way, success cannot be measured in a vacuum. You need to know what you want and then set out on a journey to achieve it. Furthermore, once you know your purpose, it's easier to decide your next action. It will also help to funnel your time, energy, and effort into the things that are of importance.

One of the biggest payoffs of having a purpose is the

drive to push through towards the realization of your goals regardless of challenges and obstacles. Those who are not driven by purpose generally quit when the going gets rough. Take R. U. Darby for example. In Napoleon Hill's bestselling book *Think and Grow Rich*, Napoleon tells the story of how R. U. Darby abandoned his search for buried treasure when he was just three feet from gold.[46]

Once upon a time, during the gold-rush days, Darby's uncle had gold fever, so he went digging in search of his pot of gold. After weeks of hard work, the uncle became elated when he discovered a vein of valuable ore. He quickly covered up his findings and returned home to secure the appropriate machinery to bring the ore to the surface. After sharing the news with relatives who helped him raise the money he needed for the equipment, the uncle and Darby returned to continue working the gold mine.

The first set of ore was mined and things were looking pretty good. Just when they thought they would be able to clear their debt and then make a big profit, the vein of ore disappeared. After trying feverishly to pick up the vein again they threw their hands in the air and quit. In frustration, they sold their machinery to a junk man for a few hundred dollars and went back home. While they had given up without finding the pot of goal at the end of their rainbow, the prudent junk man called in a mining engineer to take a look at the mine. Upon examining the mine, the engineer advised that the vein of gold could be picked up again just three feet from where Darby and his uncle had stopped digging. Imagine that! They were three feet from gold. So close, and yet so far!

The junk man went on to make millions of dollars from the mine. Darby, however, learned the lesson—you need to persevere through difficulties and if you do, success will be realized. The reality is that when you are driven by purpose, it becomes much easier to persevere. In addition, your payoff will be unbelievable. Be mindful, though, that before realizing success, you will be met with temporary defeat and some amount of failure.

BUILD COMPETENCE

It is impossible to be successful in any area of life without a certain level of competence. By competence, I mean having the skills or ability to do something effectively and successfully. I remember the first time I was asked to give a speech. Like many people who shake in their boots just at the thought of having to speak on a public stage, I dreaded the moment. A couple of weeks later, I walked into that little country church. Everybody was staring at me, but with a trembling voice, I managed to pull it off. I was, however, pulled aside later by one of the leaders who volunteered to help me get better at public speaking. The take-away was that I lacked competence in public speaking, and it was now obvious to me and everyone else. Today, after over 20 years of training and speaking, I consider myself to be quite competent in the speaking profession.

Competence doesn't happen overnight. It takes time and effort, but will be worth it in the long run. Therefore, understanding the process of learning a new skill can help you develop competence, and you can become a master at what you do. The Conscious Competence Model of Learning conceptualizes the process by which someone moves from learning a new skill to mastery. These four psychological states through which an individual passes, on her way to mastery, include unconscious incompetence, conscious incompetence, conscious competence, and unconscious competence.

Unconscious Incompetence

In this first stage, the model purports that "you don't know that you don't know." In other words, you do not know how to do something and you are unaware of it.

Take a moment to remember a time before you learned how to drive, a time when you were not even aware that you couldn't drive and it just didn't matter to you. This state describes your "unconscious incompetence." In order for you to move from this stage to the next, you would first have to recognize your incompetence and the value of the skill to be learned.

Conscious Incompetence

In this second stage, the idea is this: "You know that you don't know." Thus, though you do not understand or know how to do something, you are aware of it, as well as of the value of learning the new skill in addressing the deficit. Let's go back to the example of driving a car. One day you became intrigued as you saw your parents or someone else driving a car and you thought, "Hey, that looks cool! I wish I could do that!" Do you remember now how difficult it was to multitask as you tried to keep the vehicle on the road during your driver training? This experience is an example of how consciously aware you were of your incompetence.

Conscious Competence

In the conscious competence stage, "you know how to do something." However, demonstrating the skill requires concentration and effort. It may require that you break down the skills into steps and have a strong conscious involvement in the execution of the skills. As your level of competence improves, the frequency of mistakes will decline. Let's illustrate with the learning-to-drive scenario. While you were having challenges with multitasking and keeping the vehicle on the road, you persevered. Your perseverance produced results; you got better at driving to the point where you were now maneuvering the vehicle down the street. You were now competent, though still conscious of what you were doing.

Unconscious Competence

In this fourth and final stage, "you know how to do something instinctively." In other words, you have had so much practice with the skill that it has now become second nature and can be performed easily. Let's go back to driving. In this stage you are all ready for school or work and you just jumped into your car, turn on the ignition, step on the gas pedal, and off you go. Everything just seems to happen effortlessly. You are now oblivious to all the coordination that once demanded your attention to keep the car on the road. You are now unconsciously competent in driving a car.

Building competence, therefore, requires you to accept and follow these four steps as you move from being a novice to becoming more competent at what you do. Tuning into your purpose will, therefore, set you on a path towards developing your competence and the success you desire.

Chapter 5

LET YOUR PASSION FUEL YOU

"A person can succeed at almost anything for which they have unlimited enthusiasm" ~ Charles M. Schwab

Wherever you find purpose, you will generally find passion. While purpose is about a cause to which one feels called, passion is an inner-drive to fulfill one's purpose. It is a deeply-felt feeling of enthusiasm and excitement that motivates you towards the fulfillment of your calling. As gasoline is to a car's engine, so is passion to your success. In essence, a person's courage to fulfill his/her vision comes from passion. But what does passion have to do with success? How does staying focused impact success? How may mastering your craft affect your success? Let's find out!

PASSION AND SUCCESS

Successful people are passionate about succeeding. This is because they love what they do. They also have a passion for their field, whether it's in sports or business. If you are to succeed in any field, you will need passion. Here's why! Success will never be realized without frustration. The major difference between those who fail and those who succeed is the desire to keep going during times of difficulty. Those who lack passion will quit, while those who are fueled by passion will go around or climb over obstacles.

I almost quit during my first year in college. In the fall of 1991, I started college with enough money to cover room, board, and tuition for the first semester. Towards the end of the semester, I was reminded that in order for me to register for the next semester, I had to pay at least 50% of the cost up front. Quite frankly, I didn't have it! "Was this the end of the road for me?" I pondered.

I remember sitting alone one day under an almond tree near the college's playing field, just thinking about my life. I talked with myself about where I was coming from and where I wanted to go. The conversation was punctuated with fear, tears, sadness, hope, and despair. After a while, I dried my tears, sat up straight on the bench, and told myself, "You didn't come all this way only to quit now." Refocusing on my purpose reignited my passion, and I decided then and there that nothing was going to prevent me from fulfilling my calling. Since then, my passion has been fueling me.

Passion is something you love, something that gets you excited. People with passion spur themselves on toward massive success and a life of meaning and fulfillment. When you love what you do, you will be more inventive and it will ultimately bring out the greatness within you. A large percentage of people in the world today do not love what they do. Some even hate their jobs, but keep doing it because it pays the bills. This is tragic! As Marsha Sinetar suggested in her book *Do What You Love, The Money Will Follow*, we are meant to work in ways that are meaningful to us as we express ourselves and serve others.[48] The bottom-line is this: successful people's achievement is intricately linked to the joy and passion they have and experience from what they do.

One of the questions I get asked by a lot of people, whether in workshops or during a one-on-one coaching session, is this: "How long before I start seeing results?" Most of us tend to ask this question when we are about to pursue a career or goal in life, don't we? The reality, though, is that success takes time. People who are fueled by passion keep going because they love what they do and are prepared to invest the time and effort needed to achieve their goals. People who lack passion are easily frustrated and generally give up during difficulty. They give up what they are pursuing and try something else that they think is easier. When things don't turn out according to their expectations, they change again and again and again.

I am not in any way suggesting that if something isn't working out, you should keep doing it. That's insanity. What I am suggesting is that you embrace the fact that there will be a waiting period—a period during which you will need to become curious, when you are tempted to become frustrated. Unlike people who don't love what they do, those who love what they do will evaluate, change course, or persist in their efforts. With that kind of drive, they are almost guaranteed success. In other words, they let their passion fuel them through their obstacles as they pursue their purpose.

Therefore, if you are to tune into your purpose, you have to identify where you are holding back in your life and let go. Feel the energy that moves you; tap into it; let it fuel you in the direction you feel called. As you do, participate with your whole heart and allow yourself to be a channel of positive change to the world as you step into your greatness.[49]

LEARN TO FOCUS

It is true that you can do anything you set your mind to, but it is also equally true that it is not physically possible for you to do everything you want to do. If that is the case, you have to stop doing everything if you want to do anything. This means focusing on one thing at a time. You can, of course, be a jack of all trades, but that won't serve you well if you are a master of none. As the Russian proverb suggests, "If you chase two rabbits you will not catch either one." Therefore, in order to succeed, it's important to focus on what you want and pursue it with persistence and dogged perseverance.

Michael Jordan, also known as MJ, is one of basketball's greatest players. MJ's accomplishments include leading the Chicago Bulls to six NBA championships, winning the most valuable player award five times, earning the regular-season MVP award five times, earning the all-star MVP award three times, and is thus considered the greatest basketball player of all times.[50]

Although Jordan achieved unparalleled success in his career, this basketball great also experienced failure and setback. MJ experienced failure throughout his career both at the high school and NBA levels. The first year he got to the NBA playoffs, his team, the Chicago Bulls, were eliminated in the first round. The next two years, his team lost miserably to the Boston Celtics. They later got defeated three times in a row by the Detroit Pistons, but Michael kept focused and would not surrender to defeat. You guessed right! Jordan went on to win many championships and a prominent place as a star in NBA history.

Like Jordan, if you are going to achieve greatness you have to stay focused. One of Jordan's winning qualities was that he never paid attention to the defeats or victories of the past. Instead, he stayed focused on the present—the current game. In other words, wherever you go, be there. American comedian Josh Billings advised, "Be like a postage stamp—stick to one thing until you get there."

Thus, how does one stay focused on one thing? Gary Keller suggested that you first go small. This means ignoring all the things that you could do and do the things that you should do.[51] Interestingly enough, the narrower your focus is, the more phenomenal results you have. If you had all the bricks to build a wall, how many bricks could you lay at one time? You guessed right! Only one! The wall can only be built one brick at a time. This is how success is done—you start each day by focusing on laying that brick. Just stay focused on that small task;

build momentum, create that snowball effect, and sooner or later, success will be realized. Interestingly enough, "it is those who concentrate on but one thing at a time who advance in the world."[52]

MASTER YOUR CRAFT

Having a purpose will encourage you to specialize, and specializing leads to mastery. Specialists are generally experts in their field. Put another way, "your success in life will depend a great deal on your ability to know much about a specific area and to perform exceptionally within it."[53]

As was mentioned before, to achieve any level of success, you will need to develop competence. To experience phenomenal results, though, you need to become an expert in your field through specialization. For clarification, a competent person has sufficient skills, knowledge ability or qualification, while an expert is extraordinarily capable or knowledgeable in his/her field. Therefore, being called an expert is more than just being good at something. The individual usually has an extensive knowledge of his/her field. In addressing a problem, if one skill cannot resolve the issue, the expert is able to reach for another skill to address the issue, because there are plenty of them in the "tool-box."

The biggest mistake I made in the early part of my career was trying to live a life that looked good on paper. I tried to be "jack-of-all-trades" when I should really have focused on being an expert in the area of my greatest strength. Of course, we are not generally taught the importance of mastery in school. Growing up like many of you, I was taught to fix my weaknesses, instead of dedicating my time and energy to the things that I had an affinity to. Imagine where you could have been if you had just started your journey to mastery earlier! You would have been closer to mastering what you do and living the life you have always wanted. Suffice it to say, it is still not too late to be what you can become. Just start building on your strengths and start outsourcing your weaknesses.

Throughout history, the people who attained mastery in their craft have been people who discovered their calling, mastered their mind, and practiced as a way of developing their craft.

Calling

As was mentioned in the previous chapter, a calling is a strong urge to follow a particular path. It's an inner drive that seeks to guide you towards your life's purpose. As Robert Green in his book Mastery put it, "The first move towards mastery is always inward—learning who you really are and reconnecting with that innate force."[54] This kind of inward look creates a further interest in activities that seem to align with your abilities and skills set.

Once there is clarity around this sense of calling, specialization becomes inevitable on the path to fulfilling this "call." As you seek to acquire specialized knowledge, however, first decide on the type of specialized knowledge you need and why you need it. Essentially; in order for you to master a field, you have to love it.

Ludwig Van Beethoven was a German pianist and composer and was widely regarded as the greatest composer of all time. Ludwig's father, observing his talent for the piano, tried to make him a child prodigy like Mozart, but without success. With a burning desire to realize his dream of having a prodigiously talented musician son, Johann, Beethoven's dad, developed a rigorous practice regiment in the early years of the boy's life. The results of this approach, however, were less than desirable. On March 26, 1778, Beethoven's father arranged his first public recital; he was just 7 years old. Unfortunately, the recital did not launch his musical career as his father had intended.

Like many who have tasted success, Beethoven was not exempt from life's challenges. Though his family was at one point very prosperous, they became steadily poorer after the death of his grandfather in 1773. Things got worse when his father became an alcoholic. By age 11, Beethoven had left school and by age 18, he had become the breadwinner of the family.[55]

Regardless of Beethoven's setbacks, which included deafness, his love for the piano did not wane. History has proven that this pianist, composer, and musical genius is undoubtedly the greatest of all time. Simply put, Beethoven loved what he did.

Like Beethoven, you have to love what you do, stay focused, and let your passion fuel you towards your greatness. If your desire is to be an engineer, stop spending your time learning accounting principles, unless this particular knowledge is required to enhance your being an engineer. The knowledge you need to acquire will depend to a large extent on the goal or purpose to which you are driven. Once you are settled on the purpose and the particular specialized knowledge desired, the next move is to locate the source from which this knowledge can be obtained.

People who have acquired specialized knowledge on their path to mastery have found the following sources useful:
- Personal experience

- Colleges and universities
- Books & periodicals
- Joining professional organizations
- Mentorship
- Professional development training (workshops, seminars, certification programs).

Having acquired specialized knowledge, the temptation to relax is always a present reality. Champions, however, never become preoccupied with past success; they build on it. Interestingly enough, successful men and women irrespective of their calling, never stop learning—especially in their area of expertise—as they pursue success relating to their purpose, business or profession.[56]

Control Your Mind

I was scared to death when mid-term reports were sent home to my parents. Even though I knew they couldn't read what was on my report card, it still scared me. Of the more than 20 students in my class, I was always in the bottom five when it came to failure. The only thing that was constant for me during the first four years in high school was my bad behavior and poor grades. Here is why I kept failing. I kept telling myself that my situation was permanent and could not change. It was my belief that one was either born smart or born dumb, and I concluded that I was the latter. My mind was just out of control.

The breakthrough came for me, after I saw how much my parents and the principal believed in me. This caused a seismic shift in my belief system and I started telling myself, "If the principal believes in me that much, maybe I am not that dumb after all." This simple shift came when I took control of my mind and intentionally decided what I would allow my mind to focus on. In other words, I changed my mind-set. This is what got me on a path of success that astounded even my friends and relatives.

Mindsets are just belief systems. They are powerful beliefs that shape your view of the world, the actions you take, and the results you will receive. According to mindset expert Dr. Carol Dweck, the view you hold of yourself, has a profound impact on how you live your life.[57] If you are going to realize your dream and live a fulfilled and successful life, you have no choice but to take control of your mind and resist the temptation of believing that your basic qualities and abilities are carved in stone.

Believe that you can, and you will. With that in mind, start viewing your basic qualities as things you can change if you put in the work. You may not be able to become a Beethoven, but you will become much more than who you currently are. As Douglas Malloch suggested;

> "If you can't be a highway then just be a trail,
> If you can't be the sun be a star;
> It isn't by size that you win or you fail—
> Be the best of whatever you are!"

Practice

I was recently watching a video on the life of the legend and fastest man on earth—Usain Bolt. I was astounded by the number of hours he had to put into training to run a race lasting approximately 10 seconds. Bolt is considered the greatest sprinter of all times, earning him the nickname "Lightning Bolt." His athletic feat includes being an eight time Olympic gold medalist, winning the 100 m, 200 m and 4 x 100 m relay at three consecutive Olympic Games. Bolt is also an eleven-time World Champion, winning consecutive World Championships in the 100m, 200 m, and 4 x 100 relay from 2009 to 2015 (with the exception of one 100 meter race in which he had a false start in 2011).

What got my attention during this documentary was the fact that the "fastest man" has scoliosis. Normally, the spine of an individual runs straight down the back. On the contrary, the spine (backbone) of a person with scoliosis curves to the side.[59] In an interview with ESPN in 2011, Bolt described how he managed his scoliosis through hard work and training:

> When I was younger it wasn't really a problem. But you grow and it gets worse. My spine's really curved bad [makes "S" shape with finger]. But if I keep my core and back strong, the scoliosis doesn't really bother me. So I don't have to worry about it as long as I work hard. The early part of my career, when I didn't really know much about it, it really hampered me because I got injured every year."[60]

With regular exercise that strengthened the lower back and core, Usain Bolt was able to overcome the challenge of his curved spine, becoming the greatest sprinter of all times. Usain Bolt's training routine includes spending 90 minutes at the gym every day. His daily workouts are geared towards improving speed and agility while maintaining a sculpted and athletic body. To train for the 100m sprint, he divides the speed into four phases—*the starting blocks; the acceleration, top end speed and deceleration.*[61] In other words, before Bolt gets into his 10-second race, he clocks hundreds of hours of practice time. During one interview, Bolt told a reporter, "The work is behind the scenes; the competition is the easy part; behind the scenes is where the work is done, and everything is done to get to that one race that you need to run."[62] So although you may be naturally talented, you have to develop your skill through hours and hours of work, since talent can only take you so far and no further.

Therefore, it seems that the major advantage of the masters—those who are good at what they do—is more time in practice. Whether you are preparing for an exam, a game, the spelling-bee competition, or any task, for that matter, more time in practice is going to make you stand out from the rest and bring you one step closer to mastering your craft. Research suggests that "ten thousand hours of practice spread over ten years is just a rough average"[63] of what it takes to be a master in your field. Of course, some people will take less and some may even take more, but the bottom line is that in order to be great, you have to put in the work.

As I observe the lives of people like Michael Jordan, Ludwig Van Beethoven, Usain Bolt, and many more, I have come to realize that their practice was not done by happenstance; it was done with deliberate intention. Deliberate practice is a concept advanced by Anders Erickson who spent his career studying how experts become experts. Ericsson posited that though ten thousand hours of practice spread over a period of time will take your game to another level, the real game changer has to do with how you practice.[64] In other words, the quality of your practice is more important than the quantity. Like highly successful people, when you engage in deliberate practice, improving your performance over time has got to be your goal and motivation. That said, deliberate practice is different from work and it certainly isn't play. It involves repetition of a task, requires unrestraint effort, and is not inherently enjoyable. In the book Talent is Overrated, Geoff Colvin highlighted four key elements of deliberate practice:[65]

1. **Design the activity.** Design means having a clearly defined goal that stretches and pulls you to the edge of your capabilities. The best way to do this is with the help of a mentor or a coach. This is because you can't see yourself in the picture if you are in the frame.

2. **It's mentally demanding and requires full concentration and effort.** This means staying focused on the task with intense concentration. Practice, here, is not about how you feel, but more about achieving the goal.

3. **Feedback on the results of the activity is continuously available.** It isn't possible to get better without feedback. Therefore, as soon as you complete the activity, seek feedback. Don't

just look for what's wrong or even what's right; look for what's missing. Seek feedback on how to become better and even if you find something that "ain't broke, improve it."

4. **The activity must be repeated a lot.** This means doing the thing over and over again until you experience unconscious competence. If there is an area of vulnerability, it must be worked and reworked until it is mastered.

Now, do you want to hear the truth? Practice isn't always fun, but it's an invaluable investment into becoming better at what you do. Ultimately, it will bring out the greatness in you and cause you to achieve the results you desire.

Chapter 6

GETTING YOUR DREAM OFF THE LAUNCHING PAD

It always seems impossible until it's done.
~ Nelson Mandela

On the eleventh of June 1995, I graduated from college with my first degree—this was a dream come true! It was a proud moment for me as I proved her wrong! I proved to Julie, a family friend, who had told me it could not be done; that it can be done. She told me that going to college, in pursuit of a four year degree was impossible. On the contrary I told myself, "I must. I can. I will."

This self-appointed dream killer and messenger of doom reminded me, "You are not that smart and your parents are poor." She knew of some of the academic struggles I had experienced in high school and with her fixed mindset, she attempted to put a cap on my potential. For a moment I was tempted to believe her. My gremlins (mental chatter) started reminding me, "You are average! Remember, that in high school your grades were below "C" until your second year in the tenth grade. What if history repeats itself while you are in college?" Of course, by now you know what happened. I went to college, graduated after four years and proved her wrong.

I have to admit that realizing my dream wasn't easy. However, faith in a higher power and telling myself every day, "I can, I must, I will," got me through. Furthermore, I decided not to allow someone else's opinion of me to become my reality. As a matter of fact, that woman's negative words were my greatest motivation while in college.

I agree with Paul J. Meyer, founder of the Success Motivation Institute, who once said, "Whatever you vividly imagine, ardently desire, sincerely believe, and enthusiastically act upon... must inevitably come to pass!"[66] If you are to beat the odds and get your dream off the launching pad, you must first *imagine your dream*; second, *you must believe it's possible*; and third, *you must take action*.

IMAGINE YOUR DREAM

You can't have a dream come true without first having a dream. In essence, if you don't know what you want, you won't be able to achieve what you want. Your first line of duty in realizing your dream, therefore, is simply to imagine it. Walt Disney called it "imagineering."[67] This means creating a mental picture of the future based on how you would like it to be with the intention of implementing those creative ideas into practical form. Thus, in order to pursue your dream, you have to visualize it.

Though dreaming is important, you have to move past the dreaming phase to the vision phase. While a dream is what you see when you are imagining a hypothetical situation, a vision is what you see when you look to the future without hypothesizing, wishing, or imagining. In other words, a dream is a state of being occupied by one's thoughts, whereas a vision is the ability to visualize where you want to be and having a plan of action to make it happen. To put it another way, a vision is a mental picture of the future you want to create.

Imagining your dream is, consequently, the process of exploring your hopes and aspirations for your work, relationships, organization, and the world at large. It can be an energizing exploration of possibilities about what might be and the things you could create.

In creating your vision, visualize where you want to be in your lifetime, or at least, by a significant and distant period in the future. Ask yourself, "What does my ideal life look like?"

Picture it as if it has already happened. If it's a job, see yourself in the job; if it's a car, see yourself driving it. Before I started college in 1991, I saw myself graduating. I even went to a graduation ceremony at the college before I got started. Your dream is possible, but you first need to be clear on what it is you want by visualizing it.

BELIEVE IT'S POSSIBLE

On May 25, 1961, before a joint session of Congress, President Kennedy delivered a visionary speech that is considered one of the greatest speeches in history. While I am impressed with JFK's oratory and communication skills, I am fascinated by the certainty with which he shared his dream—that of one day putting man on the moon. Kennedy said this to Congress as he requested funding for this audacious goal: "First, I believe that this nation should commit itself to achieving the goal, before the decade is out, of landing a man on the moon and returning him safely to earth."[68]

Suffice it to say, on July 20, 1969, eight years after the speech, NASA's Apollo 11 mission, landed the first two humans on the moon. Mission commander Neil Armstrong's first words from the moon were breathtaking. All over the earth he was heard saying, "That's one small step for (a) man; one giant leap for mankind."[69] Although Kennedy did not live to see this breakthrough in space exploration, it was indeed a dream come true.

Believing like President Kennedy, that your dream is possible, is going to be vital in realizing that dream. In fact, if you have the courage to pursue your dream, you may just be rewarded with having them come true. Hence, once you have visualized where you want to be, your next step is to believe you can do it.

Belief is one of the most powerful and creative forces in the universe. What do I mean by belief? By believing, I mean having the certainty that the mental picture of the future that you hold in your mind, will one day be a tangible realty in the present. It is being certain that if you do what needs to be done, you will succeed. This certainty is akin to that of the White brothers who held the belief that one day they would have a flying machine—the airplane—flying through the sky. It is being certain, like JFK that one day man would land on the moon. In addition, it is being certain that whatever dream you have, it can and will come true.

Regardless of your background or your social standing, your dream is possible. So what is your dream? Is it to be a doctor, lawyer, entrepreneur, business owner, or singer? Whatever it is, your dream is valid. Remember, though, that your only obstacle is you, and to a large extent, your belief system. Hence, your success will depend to a large extent on what you believe. Of course, it would be naive not to expect obstacles and challenges as you pursue your dream, so be prepared to experience delays, hardship, and failure. This should in no way cause you to quit or give up. Just keep believing.

TAKE ACTION

Dreams do come true, but only after the dreamer wakes up. Put another way, you cannot realize your dream by just wishing; neither can you build your future on what you are going to do. You must take action now. As Thomas Henry Huxley correctly put it, "The great end of life is not knowledge but action."[70] So although believing is one of the ingredients for success, believing alone won't "cut it." You have to take action.

To get started, design a plan of action. Determine "what should be" and the strategies required for it to happen. The question that needs to be answered now, therefore, is this: "What do I need to do right now, next week, and next month to realize my dream?" Once you decide what needs to be done, you must get started. In other words, you can't win if you don't begin, and you can't finish if you don't start. So, apply for the job, start your business, apply for college or university: just start running towards your dream.

When I started college in 1991, I had tuition for only the first semester. That's it! But I started. I wasn't as smart as others, but I started. Here is the simple truth: You can't finish if you don't start! You can't earn if you don't work, and you can't succeed if you don't try. Was I afraid of failing and dropping out of college after the first semester? Sure I was! That fear did not deter me, however, so I pursued my dream; you should, too.

One of the major differences between successful people and unsuccessful people is action. They both feel the fear, but successful people take action anyway. To realize your dream, you have to be willing to take the leap, embrace failures, and learn from your mistakes. For some people, the fear of making mistakes is immobilizing. However, mistakes are inevitable, so get used to experiencing them. The German proverb sums it up perfectly: "You will become clever through your mistakes." Therefore, a mistake is feedback about what needs to be done better. It is a signal that you are off target and need to make an adjustment in order to hit the target.

Of course, you may have to adjust many times before hitting the target. In order to make your results progressively better, however, ensure that after taking *action*, you include these other three steps: review, refine, repeat as illustrated in *The Cycle of Success*.

Review

Bearing in mind that you have designed a plan and taken appropriate actions towards the achievement of your goal, reviewing your progress is the first step towards getting phenomenal results. In essence, reviewing is the process of receiving feedback on what you were supposed to do, how it was done, and the results you have received. In reviewing your progress, ask yourself the following questions:

1. Has the action achieved the goal?
2. What worked well?
3. What didn't work?
4. What was missing?
5. What can I do differently?

The reviewing process will help you keep track of the progress you have been making, so that you can refine the plan as needed for greater performance and productivity.

Refine

Once you have reviewed your progress, the next step is to go to work and refine your plan. This means improving on it. It means making the necessary changes. No plan is ever perfect at the very beginning. It will inevitably need to be fine-tuned. When you engage in the process of refining, seek to create greater clarity on what the ultimate outcome looks like. Ensure that your actions are aligned with the direction in which you need to go as you become clearer on what you want, why you want it, how to get it, and the time-line in getting it.

Repeat

Be cyclical with your approach in getting better at what you do. Having reflectively learned what worked and what did not adjust the plan to include the insights you have received from your feedback. Once you have refined your plan, repeat the process until the desired result has been achieved.

CYCLE OF SUCCESS

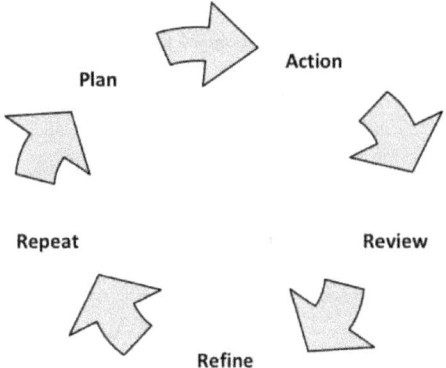

As you seek to get your dream off the launching pad and turn your ideas into reality, don't be lulled into complacency by your past success and don't become a failure because you failed, either. Don't allow obstacles, roadblocks or set-backs to deter you. Believe that your dream is possible. As a matter of fact, don't stop because you are tired, either; stop only when you are done!

Reflection

WHAT? (WHAT SPOKE TO YOU)

_____
_____
_____
_____
_____
_____
_____
_____

SO WHAT? (YOUR TAKE-AWAY)

_____
_____
_____
_____
_____
_____
_____
_____

NOW WHAT? (YOUR PLAN OF ACTION)

_____
_____
_____
_____
_____
_____
_____
_____

Part Three

NO LIMITS

Chapter 7

BEATING THE ODDS

"A champion is one who gets up when he can't"
~ Jack Dempsey

The world in which we live is constantly changing. Being constantly inundated with these changes can become overwhelming and turbulent. The secret to surviving and thriving in this era of change and turbulence is being *resilient*. The good news is that we all have an inborn predisposition to become resilient. By resilient, I mean being able to adapt and thrive during difficult life experiences. It is not just to bounce back from difficulties; it is beating the odds—using the challenge as a foundation on which to build. However, in order to build your resilience so you are able to beat the odds, you must have an "I Can," an "I must," and an "I will" approach to life.

I MUST

"If you can take it, you can make it!" This was the oft-repeated line in one of the most impactful movies about the will to survive that I have ever seen. A friend of mine, who is a neuropsychologist and clinical psychologist, recommended that I watch the movie "Unbroken" after I mentioned to her that I was doing research on resilience. Unbroken is a 2014 war film and a World War II story of survival and resilience. The movie is based on the life of U.S Olympian Louis Zamperini, portrayed in the film by Jack O'Connell.[71]

As a boy, Louis was always getting into trouble. With the help of his older brother Pete, he channeled his energy into running and eventually became an accomplished distance runner and an Olympian in the summer Olympics of 1936 in Berlin, Germany. Although he ran an astonishing race in his first Olympics, Louis was placed eighth in the 5,000 meter race. The young Italian-American from Torrance, California was eager to run in the Olympics of 1940 with the hope of winning the gold. His hope was dashed, however, when World War II ended his dream forever.

When the war broke out, Louis enlisted in the military, and in 1943, while on a search-and-rescue mission, his plane crashed in the Pacific Ocean. For days Louis and his fellow soldiers—Phil and Mac—endured "hell" on a raft that drifted aimlessly at sea. As the "boys" battled the elements and struggled to survive hunger, heat, cold, and the psychological isolation of being stranded on a raft in enemy territory, Louis kept telling himself, "If you can take it you can make it." Unlike Louis who became resilient during this "hellish" ordeal, the fear of encroaching death broke the spirit of Mac who kept telling the others, "We are going to die." Guess what happened? He died some time later, just as he had said.

On the contrary, Louis' indomitable spirit kept him going, and after a grueling 47 days adrift on a shark-encircled life raft, he and his friend Phil were captured by the Japanese as Prisoners of War (POW). Though they went on to experience mind-blowing cruelty in the Japanese POW camps, they eventually survived and lived to tell their story. Louis had an "I Must" attitude.

Singer and song writer Kelly Clarkson said in one of her songs, "What doesn't kill you makes you stronger."[72] Incidentally, what doesn't kill you can make some people weaker too. The differentiating factor between those who beat the odds and thrive during difficulties and those who don't is purpose, self-motivation, and self-actualization.

Purpose

Being driven by purpose is the energy that fuels individuals, organizations, and businesses towards the fulfillment of their ideals. A person who has purpose in their life has direction, something to live for, and meaning—a reason for being. Viktor Frankl called it your "why" in his book *Man's Search For Meaning*.[73]

Purpose has a way of pulling us into the future. According to Jim Rohn in one of his many speeches on personal development, we have to deal with many influences on a daily basis. The influence of the past pulls some people back into the past, while others are pulled aside by the distraction of the distractions. Purpose, on the other hand, pulls you towards the future, as well as pulling you through your challenges and difficulties.[74]

Over the years, I have admired and listened to successful people tell their stories about their success. I have discovered one thing they all have in common: they know why they are here. Their life is driven by purpose. But how does one identify his or her purpose? Here are three ways to find out.

1. Define Your Core Values

The first step in identifying your purpose is to define your core values. We are the embodiment of the values we espouse. Take Martin Luther King Jr., for example. In his short, but inspiring life, he made an incredible impact on the landscape of American society and the world at large. Dr. King believed in justice, equality, and freedom for all. These were some of his core values. These values enabled him to align himself with his purpose—that of leading the cause of the civil rights movement.

Like Dr. King, once you can define your core values, you will be one step closer to finding your purpose. So what do you stand for? What centers you? What principles guide your decisions and behavior? If you can answer these questions in the affirmative you have laid the foundation for identifying your purpose and are on the path to living life to the fullest. Here is what I want you to do right now! Take a sheet of paper and list your top ten core values. Go over your top ten list and identify and define your top five core values. Once you have defined those five core values, start exploring activities, causes, and/or careers that you feel are in alignment with your values.

2. Discover Your Passion

Passion is the genesis of greatness! It is what you love to do and the force that will awaken the giant in you. Like identifying your core values, discovering your passion will help you find your purpose in life. So what are you passionate about? What gets you excited? What is it that wakes you up in the morning and keeps you up at nights with excitement? That particular thing may just be an indication of the purpose for which you were born.

I have to admit, however, that passion alone is not a safe guide in determining your purpose. As my mentor John Maxwell put it, passion is not 100% foolproof, but it will get you within the location and the neighborhood where you will find your purpose. That is, it is possible to be passionate about something you are not good at. I used to watch *American Idol*, an American singing competition television series, as contestants auditioned for the show with the hope of one day becoming a star. Some of the aspiring singers auditioned with exuberance, but honestly, it was clear they couldn't sing. They were passionate about singing, but passion alone wasn't enough. It was obvious they would be better off pursuing another career. Suffice it to say, passion is a very important factor in the process of finding your purpose, but understand that it's about 80% accurate and must be associated with your skills-set if you are to find and live your purpose.

3. Identify Your Skills

Intricately linked to what you are passionate about is what you are good at. In other words, "what is your area of competence?" That being said, one of the most important questions to ask as you try to find your purpose is this: "What are my strengths?" Try to identify what you do well. This means identifying your giftedness and your unique skills set. Bear in mind that until you go out and try several things you won't have a good idea what you are good at and what you enjoy. Once you have identified your core values, your area of passion, and your strengths (your skills and that thing that you are good at), just go ahead and live your life with purpose.

Self-motivation

Whether you are a student, leader, entrepreneur, or just launching your career, your success will depend a lot on how well you can motivate yourself. Once there is a conviction about the reason for which a person or a business exists, passion, an unquenchable desire, is born. This is usually accompanied by a strong commitment to achieving and realizing one's set goals. In other words, purpose drives internal motivation, which drives performance—critical factors in succeeding and maintaining success in the long run. As a matter of fact, if you are going to perform at your best, you must first be self-motivated.[75]

This self-motivated characteristic has always been a part of the lives of those who have beaten the odds. As a matter of fact, "highly resilient people know they can count on themselves during rough times."[76] The choice is yours; therefore; be miserable or motivate yourself. Never depend on external conditions to motivate you; it won't last. By external, I mean money, rewards, or even encouragement from others. Though these may help, they do not guarantee you the level of motivation required to thrive during difficulties.

Abraham Lincoln is considered one of the greatest United States Presidents and one of the best examples of someone who beat the odds through persistence and self-motivation. Born into poverty, Lincoln experienced difficulties throughout his life. He lost eight elections, failed twice in business, and once suffered a nervous breakdown.

In 1816, Lincoln's family was forced out of their home and he had to work to support them. In 1818, his mother died. In 1831, he failed in business. In 1832, he ran for State legislature and lost. In 1833, he borrowed money from a friend to start a business, but became bankrupt by the end of the year. In 1835, he became engaged to be married, but was heartbroken when his sweetheart died. In 1836, he had a nervous breakdown and spent the next six months in bed. In 1838, he sought to become speaker of the State legislature, but was defeated. In 1843, he ran for Congress and lost. In 1846, he ran for Congress again, and won, then ran again for re-election in 1843, but lost. In 1849, he sought the job of land officer in his home state of Illinois, but was rejected. In 1854, he ran for Senate of the United States and lost. In 1856, he sought the Vice-Presidential nomination at his party's national convention, but got less than 100 votes. In 1858, he ran again for U.S. Senate and lost again. In 1860, Abraham Lincoln beat the odds and was elected president of the United States.[77]

Like many others, Lincoln could have quit during the many times that he experienced failure and difficulties. Lincoln didn't give up, however, because he was driven from the inside. He kept persevering, beating the odds, and eventually, became one of the greatest presidents in the history of the United States.

Listen! If Lincoln can do it, you can do it, too. Here are three things you can do to develop and nurture your self-motivation:

1. Keep Your Goal in Mind

Having compelling goals is one of the most powerful sources of motivation. One of the things that have kept me going over the years is the drive I get from my audacious goals. Setting goals to beat poverty and get an education was what motivated me the most in my life. There were times when I experienced failures, lost friends, lost support, went broke, and became discouraged with the thought of giving up. But guess what! I chose not to quit because my goals kept creating an inner drive that fueled me forward towards my destiny.

I like how Tony Robbins put it when he said, "Goals take you beyond your limits to a world of unlimited power." As human beings, we are goal-oriented; that's how we were wired. We get tremendous pleasure from achieving our goals. Whenever we set and achieve big audacious goals, it gives us a sense of accomplishment and serves as a way of motivating us as we set new goals and pursue them. By setting goals, you are attempting to test and go beyond your limits. If these goals are inspiring and meaningful, you will develop the self-motivation and inspiration to cut through obstacles and climb over barriers in pursuit of them. Your attitude will consequently be one of fight, instead of flight.

2. Be Optimistic

Is the glass half-full or half-empty? It depends on who is answering! You may have come across this over-used illustration about optimism before. Well! You guessed right! I am going to ask you again. What is your answer? If you answered half full, you may be a person with an optimistic view of life. By optimism, I mean having a positive outlook on life. While pessimists are those who expect bad things to happen to them, optimists are individuals who expect good things to happen in their lives.

Remember Louis and Mac in "Unbroken?" Louis had an optimistic outlook. He repeatedly told himself, "If you can take it, you can make it." Mac however, with his pessimistic outlook, kept telling himself and the others that he was going to die, and that's exactly what happened to him. Here is the bottom-line: "Optimism and pessimism both tend to be self-fulfilling prophecies."[79]

So how does one develop optimism? The best way is to make a choice to be optimistic and to practice thinking differently every day. If you become frustrated by the things that are not going well in your life, rather than focusing on them, get curious and think in terms of possibilities. This is because we generally make greater potential of what we focus on. Furthermore, "if you expect a good outcome, your brain spots little events and momentary opportunities that can lead to that outcome"[80] and will ultimately set you up for success.

3. Remain Hopeful

People who feel hopeful increase their chances of growing through the difficulties they encounter in life. While optimism is the belief that you will have good positive experiences in the future, hope is a positive motivational state that accepts reality with an attitude that refuses to quit.[81]

When we need a booster shot of motivation to get us pass our hurdles so that we may reach our goals, hope never fails. Hope also has a way of giving us a reality check. It makes us challenge our present reality in a rational way. By so doing, you may realize that the things you worry about are not life-or-death issues as you previously thought. For example, what is the worst that can happen if you start your own business? You can either meet with amazing success or you can learn what needs to be improved. In other words, the world won't end if you bet on yourself. To have hope, therefore, signals the quest for new possibilities, especially when you have to deal with uncertainties. Consequently, hope keeps getting up when she falls and never stops until she wins.

Self-actualization

The term "self-actualization" is a concept in psychology regarding "the motivation to realize one's own maximum potential and possibilities."[782] The concept was originally introduced by Kurt Goldstein, a physician who specialized in neuroanatomy and psychiatry. Goldstein believed that self-actualization is the ultimate goal of human beings and that our behaviours and drives are manifestations of this motivation.[83]

According to American psychologist Abraham Maslow who popularized the concept, self-actualization is the fulfillment of one's greatest potential. However, this can only occur once a variety of other basic needs have been met.[84] Maslow's Hierarchy of Needs, proposed in his 1943 paper "A Theory of Human Motivation" postulates that our actions are motivated based on our desire to achieve certain needs. This is depicted in the pyramid below:

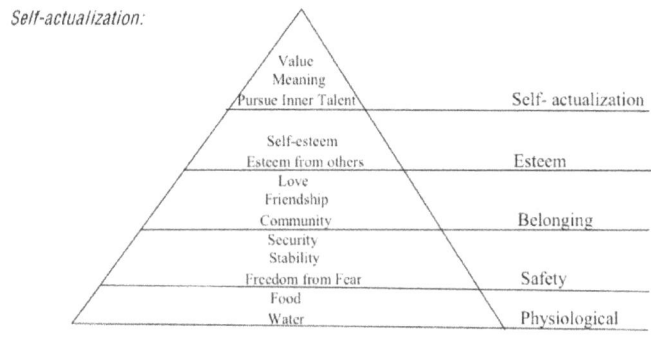

Maslow's Hierarchy of Needs

The lowest level of the pyramid is made up of our *basic needs*, while growth needs, the most complex of the needs, are located at the top. Once the lower needs are met people move up the pyramid towards the highest level—*self-actualization*. Suffice it to say, self-actualized people are constantly seeking to understand themselves by answering questions such as, "What am I about?" "Why am I here? "What's my potential?" They do this in a quest for meaning and with the goal of being the best they are potentially capable of becoming. That said, in order to be truly happy, a speaker needs to speak, a writer needs to write, and you need to unshackle your potential and live your best life now. This is the reason successful people succeed. They live with meaning, are driven from within, are guided by their values, and cannot be stopped because they are self-actualized.

I CAN

In 2008, Barak Obama's presidential campaign rallied supporters with the inspiring slogan, "Yes We Can." It was a speech that appealed to the inner-strength of the American people and a rallying call for change. As Obama left office in 2017, he called on the American people to keep believing. As he put it, "I am asking you to believe. Not in my ability to bring about change – but in yours."[85] He then concluded his speech by saying:

"Yes We Can.
Yes We Did.
Yes We Can."[86]

For Obama, "Yes we can" became "Yes we did." In order for you to experience success like Obama and others, it's important to develop an attitude that will transform your "I Can't" to "I Can." People with this kind of attitude generally create strategies that will assist them in accessing the self-generating power required to thrive in the midst of challenges as they pursue the realization of their dream. Some of the strategies that will aid you include developing a growth mindset, practicing Appreciative Inquiry (AI) and building connections of support.

Developing a Growth Mindset

In the groundbreaking work of Stanford University psychologist Carol Dweck, research has shown that achievement and success are intricately linked to our mindset. What this means is that the life you live is profoundly impacted by the view you hold about yourself.[87] Dweck's research has distinguished two perspectives that people hold about their abilities: a fixed mindset or a growth mindset.

People with a fixed mindset believe their basic qualities

(e.g. intelligence) are fixed. Those people hold the belief that their quality is carved in stone and that intelligence is fixed and cannot change. People with a fixed mindset generally avoid challenges, since failure is viewed as a lack of intelligence. Furthermore, getting feedback is negative and is viewed as criticism.

Unlike the fixed mindset, people with a growth mindset believe their basic qualities and abilities (e.g. intelligence, talent) can be developed through hard work and dedication. They believe basic qualities can be cultivated through effort and that intelligence can be developed. Individuals with a growth mindset embrace challenges as growth opportunities and see failure as problems that must be faced. In addition, these individuals usually see getting feedback as something positive that serves as a catalyst for growth and further improvement. In essence, people with a growth mindset view effort as a worthwhile path to mastering their craft.

Therefore, developing a growth mindset therefore requires that you make a mental shift in how you view your abilities. This means actively taking the stance that your abilities are not carved in stone, and that they are capable of being changed through persistent effort. Such an approach creates motivation and improves productivity and performance, be it in life, career, or business. Thus, no matter what your abilities are or how gifted you may or may not be, "effort is what ignites that ability and turns it into accomplishment."[88]

Practicing Appreciative Inquiry

Appreciative inquiry is a solution-focused approach that seeks to discover and explore the best in people and organizations. Its concern is on what is working well, why it's working well, with a focus on doing more of what's working well. In other words, AI recommends solving a problem by giving attention, not to what is wrong, but to what is right. This is because when we pay attention to problems, we emphasize them.

This change management approach, developed by David Cooperrider,[89] is generally used for organizations experiencing rapid change or growth. While this approach is useful within an organizational context, it pays high dividends when applied to our individual lives. *Appreciative* can be defined as valuing and recognizing the best in people, or the world around us, as well as affirming past and present strengths, successes, and potentials. *Inquiry*, on the other hand, is the act of exploration and discovery through questions while being open to seeing new potentials and possibilities. Therefore, AI is based on the principle that people and organizations change in the direction in which they inquire.

Suffice it to say, the questions we ask and the things we focus on indicate the importance we give them. In essence, we create more of what we focus on. However, AI offers an alternative by focusing on what is working and the desired future state. Unlike problem solving, which focuses on what's broken or not working well, AI focuses on the positives and leverages them to correct the negatives. Then how can you use AI to create success in your personal life and career? The following recommendations can be utilized as you seek the success you desire in your personal and professional life:

1. Focus on the positive and look at the particular situation through the lens of positivity.
2. Ask questions that cause you to reflect on personal stories of success.
3. Ask questions that get you thinking about your desired future.
4. Search for innovative and creative ways to create that future.

Here are a few questions to get started as you seek to grow in your career, personal, or professional life:

1. What can I do today that will help me to grow professionally?
2. How may I manage my time better during the

day for greater productivity?
3. What skills or strengths do I possess that have made me successful in my career or life so far?
4. What actions will I take today that will help me in realizing my dream?
5. What was a win I had last week?

Building Connections of Support

Connection is the state of being related to someone or something. To be connected to someone means closeness and relationship. As human beings, we exist in relationships, we are healed in relationship, and we thrive in relationship. Whether in business or in our personal lives, we cannot become fruitful and productive without relationships. Likewise, resilient people are those who build connections through meaningful relationships. The relationship could be with family, friends, employees, or an employer.

In June 2011, I walked down the aisle after 4 years of hard academic labor and received a doctoral degree, the first of its kind in my family. Just one year earlier, I had decided to throw in the towel and call it quits. Here's why! I had worked on my doctoral dissertation for about a year, only to be told by my advisor that I had to do it all over again. I had given up sleep, given up social activities, given up family time, and had even taken a one month sabbatical with 4 weeks' vacation to get this final requirement for the doctoral degree ready. My advisor, after reading through this scholarly essay, informed me that my work was of poor quality and would not meet the academic standards of the University.

I have to admit that I was angry, discouraged, and depressed at getting this daunting news. Thus, I decided to abandon four years of hard work and give up on my dream of graduating with a doctoral degree. I informed my family of my decision, with tears in my eyes, but they would have none of it. My wife hugged me and with an encouraging voice said, "You are not a quitter, you are going to do whatever it takes to get the job done and I am here to support you." The bombshell, however, came when I heard my daughter blurt out from where she was sitting on the living room couch, "Daddy, no quitting! That's what you tell us all the time! You can do it, Daddy! You can do it!"

Just hours earlier, I was planning to give up on my dream due to an unforeseen obstacle, but within seconds I decided to get back on the "horse," all because of my connections of support. With the encouraging words and support from my family, I got to work and rewrote the dissertation, which I was told, was one of the best written in that particular academic year. My family saved the day by their non-judgmental support and saw me graduate with a doctoral degree after much hard work and sacrifice.

According to the American Psychological Association, good relationships with close family members, friends, or others are important. Hence accepting help and support from those who care about you and who will listen to you, will strengthen your resolve and get you through your challenges when the going gets tough.

I WILL

In order for you to win, you have to make a decision that you will. In other words, you must have a desire to win; then create strategies to win and then, believe you will win. The "I will" attitude is a psychological stance that has the body subjected to the mind. It is a state of mind that advances regardless of the challenges and obstacles placed in your path, until the desired results have been realized. However, if your "I will" approach to life is going to bring you results, you must identify your goals, be persistent, and celebrate your success regularly.

Identify Goals

Successful people set goals and work towards achieving them. Furthermore, if you do not know where you are going, you may end up where you don't want to be. According to one study done by Gail Matthews at Dominican University, people with goals achieve more than people without goals. Respondents in the study who had written goals accomplished significantly more than those who did not have written goals. This is because goals keep you accountable, help to keep you on track, and assist you in tracking progress made. Therefore, the verdict is that writing your goals down will significantly impact your achievement.[92]

Resilient people, therefore, have goals—personal, career, and relationship. These goals help to move you from the "I can" to the "I will." However, the first step in creating a goal is to create a vision. Based on the vision that you conceptualized earlier in chapter 6, take it and turn it into a written list of concrete long-term goals. Break these long-term goals down into small targets that you must hit in order to reach your lifetime goal (say the next 3-5 years). The important thing here is to WRITE THEM DOWN! Remember, people who write their goals down are more likely to achieve them than those who don't.

To give balance to your life, try to set goals in areas such as financial, professional, emotional, relational, physical, and spiritual. Do so by asking yourself this question: "What do I want to achieve in the next 3-5 years?"

Be Persistent

Oak trees can grow to a lofty height of 65 to 100 feet and 9 feet in width. The mighty oak is a symbol of strength and endurance with a life span of over 200 years. How would you fell such a giant organism of the "tree kingdom" if all you possess is a small tool with a bladed head mounted crosswise on a handle, commonly referred to as an axe? You guessed right! One chop at a time. If you persistently take five chops at the trunk every day, over an extended period of time, the mighty oak will eventually topple to the ground.

Success is just like felling an oak tree. If you are consistently persistent, you will inevitably realize success by taking the right action every day. As Napoleon Hill once said, "Patience, persistence and perspiration make an unbeatable combination for success."[93] The power of the will is what generally drives persistence. The will to be and the will to doggedly pursue your goal by taking the right action every day until it has been achieved. Quite frankly, "without persistence, you will be defeated, even before you start. With persistence you will win."[94]

The Japanese saying, "Fall seven times, rise eight," reminds me of an experiment my daughter Akilah, brought home from school one day. The "How Green Is Your Thumb" class assignment got off to a rocky start. She had been given two seeds to plant, and she intended to make sure all the necessary conditions were met for their growth. Unfortunately, after five weeks, the seeds had not sprouted, a process that should have taken approximately two weeks. However, Akilah pushed through the frustration of her seeds' not growing, got two more seeds, replanted them, watered the soil, and exposed them to whatever sunlight she could find near the patio door in the midst of winter. After week 14, the seeds had grown to Akilah's satisfaction. Although she was successful in growing her seeds, she admitted, when submitting her project, "I find that trying to grow a plant at this time of year is very difficult." I would add, "Difficult, but not impossible."

My daughter's approach to her class assignment was persistence in a nutshell. In order to win in life, you just have to keep going even when things are difficult and appear hopeless. There have been times in my career and professional life, when I got discouraged. I had watched other less qualified people get "promoted" before me. I had made financial investments in business and failed. I had planned for things to go one way, and to my shock and chagrin, they went another way. During these moments, I would say to myself, "Throw in the towel and quit." My will to succeed however, kicked in and persistence seized the moment and got me back on track, telling me, "Just keep working, learn from your mistakes and one day it will work out."

Two of my favorite Robert Schuller quotes that have boosted my "I Will" approach to life are "Tough times don't last, tough people do"[95] and "If it's going to be, it's up to me."[96] You will, indeed, experience setbacks as you run towards your dream, but if you can wrap your mind around the idea that "this too shall pass," you will not abandon your dream. Likewise, if you take the stance that "what happens in life is largely under your control,"[97] you will discover that rather than discouraging you, your failures will fuel you.

Therefore, persistence is a state of mind that can be cultivated by living on purpose, staying hungry, believing in your capability, having a plan, and developing a daily habit of staying focused and on task. With this kind of approach to life, you will be able to climb over your fear and failures. As Napoleon Hill put it, "Those who pick themselves up after defeat and keep on trying, arrive; and the world cries, Bravo! I knew you could do it!"[98]

Celebrate Success

Whenever you realize a goal or achieve success, take time to celebrate. Absorb the implications of the success achieved and observe the progress you have made.

All of this helps you to build self-confidence and prepares you to take on future challenges. Furthermore, winning has a positive effect on one's mental state and morale.

Celebrating victories, therefore, reinforces the positive outcomes experienced, builds momentum, highlights desired actions, and gets you in the frame of mind to stay the course and succeed. Research by Harvard's Teresa Amabile on motivational levels of people on their job found that one of the greatest motivators in life is progress. When people shine a light on the progress they have made in their line of work by celebrating success, they feel motivated and develop a sense of satisfaction that enriches their lives.

Celebrating success, therefore, shifts the lens you use to view the world from "I can't" to "I can." It is a decision to divorce the impossible as you embrace the possible. Consequently, when you celebrate your wins, you are divorcing the story of your limitations as you marry the reality of your unlimited possibilities. Why don't you just pause right now and think about three wins you have experienced within the past week, month, or year and decide on a time this week when you will celebrate that success? If you do this long enough, you may begin to notice that you start attracting greater success and satisfaction in your life and work.

Chapter 8

PUSH YOURSELF TO THE NEXT LEVEL

In each of us there are places we have never gone.
Only by pressing the limits do you ever find them.
~ Joyce Brothers

So now that I've told you, "You can, you must and you will," what's next? A lot! Did you think you were just going to find your pot of gold at the end of the rainbow and just kick back and relax? You can, of course! But greatness has no limits and will not sit in a rocking chair of comfort and ease after realizing a certain level of success. Maintaining success requires that you push yourself to the next level. This means pushing yourself beyond what you think you can do and becoming better today than what you were yesterday. You can do this by practicing awareness, raising your standard, and living on the edge of your capability.

PRACTICING AWARENESS

Awareness is the pre-requisite for change. You cannot change what you are not aware of. No matter who we are or where we are from, we all want to be successful. Though each of us defines success differently, we all want to know how to be a success and have a desire to make progress in our lives. This could mean achieving greater satisfaction in a relationship, getting a promotion on the job, losing weight, or becoming financially free. While there is no single secret to success, successful people keep asking themselves three awareness questions that you also must ask if you are to be successful in your life, career or business in the long run.

Where Am I?

The first question, "Where am I?" is a question of introspection that is vitally important in assessing your current position. Without knowing where you are, you won't know how far you have come and how much farther you need to go. Socrates' famous statement, "Know thyself," becomes relevant here. Hence, when you get a grip on who you are, along with your "personal thinking patterns, you can 'get under the hood' of your vehicle and change old unwanted habits"[100] that may be holding you back.

Let's be frank! You may not like where you are, but it's important for you to be honest with yourself and accept the reality of your current status. Though you may not be very impressed with where you are, you can only "become who you are by learning who you are."[101]

Where Am I Going?

The second question, "Where am I going?" is a vision-casting question. You need to have a vision of where you want to be. It is a place or position that is, of course, much better than where you currently are. No matter how good things appear to be, they can be better. Put another way, my best today is my best today. As a matter of fact, my best today should be the foundation on which I build a better tomorrow. Consequently, you should not rest on the best, since your best is only for the moment.

"Where am I going?" is, therefore, vision-casting or vision-recasting. It is becoming consciously aware of where you are heading and ensuring that you are heading in the direction that you want to go. Suffice it to say, if you don't decide where you are heading, you may end up somewhere you didn't want to be. Therefore, the evidence is clear; you cannot achieve your best unless you have a vision of where you want to be by asking the question, "Where am I going?"

How Will I Get There?

"How will I get there?" is a powerful awareness question that pertains to the strategies and resources required to get from your current position to the future one. It involves setting a series of small goals with corresponding action-steps which must be taken consistently every day in order to achieve your desired outcome.

It is often said that a goal is a dream with a deadline. Hence, the "how will I get there?" question demands that you create a plan—a road map,[102]—to get you to where you are going. The plan should consist of your goal, strategies to achieve those goals, timelines for achieving the goals, and resources for reaching the goals. During this process, you may want to enlist the services of a coach or mentor, as these professionals have proven time and time again to be an asset to the success of those who have reached the top of their game.

Begin practicing awareness by setting aside 15 – 20 minutes each day, preferably before bed time. Look back over the activities of the day and check to see if what you had set out to do got done as planned. Don't do this in a judgmental way, but instead be curious. Think about what can be added to get better tomorrow.

Finally, as you come up with your individual answers to the three awareness questions, remember that success doesn't happen overnight. It happens by taking consistent action, maintaining an optimistic mindset, and learning from your mistakes as you pursue your goal(s).

RAISE YOUR STANDARD

Standards are the values and behaviors we hold ourselves to. Raising your standard will radically change your life and blow the cap off your capacity. By raising your standard, I mean expecting more of yourself. The higher our standards, the more productive our lives will be. Have you ever thought about the effect your personal standards have been making on your health, relationships, and personal and professional life? It is foolish to do the same thing over and over again and expect a different result. Hence, if you want to change the result, you must change the action. Consequently, in order for you to have what you have never had, you have to do the things you have never done. Simply put, you have to raise your standard! Here's how you do it!

1. Consider the Cost of Complacency

Winning can make you a slacker. This "I have arrived" attitude can deposit you in a place of complacency, causing you to slack off on your training, your diet, your work-out, and the investment in your continual growth. In raising your standard, therefore, think about what life would be like if you stayed where you are or if you pursued new dreams, new goals, and new aspirations. In other words, will I be better off tomorrow if I stay where I am or will I be better off a year or two from now if I pursue new possibilities?

If you are to move from good to great, average to phenomenal, you have to be intentional about being better today than you were yesterday. You just can't be complacent because complacency is the enemy of achievement. In today's competitive global village, those who have grown complacent or are finding it difficult to maintain their competitive edge will fail in business, their career, and life. Staying aware, setting new goals, and pursuing new horizons can be a great antidote for complacency and will consequently lead you to live a more satisfying life.

2. Change Your "Shoulds" into "Musts"

The first step in getting to any destination is making a decision to get there. Although success requires that you make a decision, taking action is usually a challenge for most people. The secret to taking action so that you might get to your destination is simply changing your "shoulds" to "musts."[103] I should pay down my debt, I should start a business, I should go to the gym are all wishful thinking. They lack the impetus and drive to get you moving. In other words, "shoulds" are just good intentions without a corresponding commitment to action.

What happens when you shift your thinking from "I should" to "I must"? Things change and success becomes inevitable. When you change your "shoulds" to "musts," you take control of the direction in which your life goes. The position you now hold is this: "I will either find a way or make a way." Let's say you have been struggling with losing weight because of the lack of commitment to your plan to exercise and eat healthy? Although you have a gym membership, you do not work-out as often as you wished. Although you have a diet plan to eat healthier, you still don't follow through. Now let's say you have a mild heart attack and your doctor tells you that if you do not make a change in your diet and lose weight, you will have another heart attack and die. As you reflect on the words of the doctor, you make a decision to change, turning your "shoulds" into "musts" because you want to be alive to see your 2- and 3-year-old daughters grow up. "I must lose weight" and "I must eat healthier" now become a primary focus and you are consequently driven like you have never been before in order to become healthy.

Thus, when you raise your standard by changing your "shoulds" to "musts," your focus and behavior will change. You will no longer settle for complacency; neither will you settle for "someday I will." Instead, you will decide, "I am going to do this now!"

GET BETTER

Self-improvement is important for continued success. If you are going to stay relevant and be your "best self," you must seek to be better every day. To get better is to improve your capacity, your ability to get a job or task done. In other words, if you are to have more or do more, you will have to become more. Indeed, "the future belongs to those who learn more skills and combine them in creative ways."[104]

In order for you to raise your standard and get better at what you do, you need to embrace the fact that your capacity is not set in stone. Hence, changing your capacity is required to becoming better as you seek to climb greater heights and pursue greater possibilities. I concur with John Maxwell who suggests that in order to change our capacity, we must first recognize that we have many capacities.[105] Here are three of John Maxwell's capacities which I believe can significantly improve your level of success if developed.

Energy Capacity[107]

This is the ability to keep going physically, with an emphasis on managing your energy rather than your time. As Jim Loehr and Tony Schwartz asserted in the book The Power of Full Engagement, "Energy, not time, is the fundamental currency of high performance." Learning to be master of your time is, therefore, important in improving your energy capacity, and ultimately, your performance and productivity.

Emotional Capacity[108]

This is about effectively managing your emotions. People who are good at managing their emotions are generally more productive, since they possess the ability to handle criticism, change and adversity well. Emotionally intelligent people do not spend time beating themselves up. Although they may not have control over how they feel, they take control over what they will do about their feelings. Improving your emotional capacity will consequently also improve your productivity.

People Capacity[109]

This is the ability to build relationships. It is in keeping with the African proverb that says, "If you want to go fast, go alone. If you want to go far, go together." Nurturing your relationships and spending time with people who will stretch you is an asset if you are going to move beyond your current level of achievement. This is because your potential, to a great extent, is determined by those with whom you spend most of your time.

As you seek to get better, do so by facing your fears, learning from your mistakes, growing professionally, investing in yourself, living with intentionality, and always thriving to be better today than you were yesterday.

LIVING ON THE EDGE OF YOUR CAPABILITY

Life is not just about living. It's about living well. It's about living your best life possible. To do that, you have to be willing to push yourself beyond your self-imposed limits. That is why I refuse to put limits on myself. As a matter of fact, I live each day with the determination to see how far I can go, and you should, too. History is prolific with the accomplishments of those who push themselves through incredible physical and mental pain to achieve some of the most significant achievements this world has ever seen. In essence, in order to keep being great at what you do, you have to live at the edge of your capability, by practicing at your edge, staying true to your call, and learning how to embrace pain.

Practice at Your Edge

Jim Collins opened his book *Good to Great* with the statement, "Good is the enemy of great."[110] He suggests that only a few people are able to attain a great life simply because it is so easy to settle for just a good life. This is in keeping with the popular saying, "If it ain't broke, don't fix it." What this means is that if something is working, you should leave it alone. In essence, be satisfied with where you are; just remain good. The question, though, is this: Why settle for good when you can be great? Why settle for average when you can be phenomenal? With this in mind, our approach to life should be, "If it ain't broke, continue to improve it."

In order for you to move from good to great, you have to learn to practice at the edge of your capability. Your edge is the highest point of your ability. Suffice it to say, it isn't a point beyond your capability. It is that mental, physical, or professional place where you experience tension from stretching yourself beyond what you currently do. To put it another way, it is looking further ahead into your own future.[111]

It is getting out of your comfort zone so that you may grow. As a matter of fact, growth requires that you be out of your comfort zone. Practicing at your edge may, therefore, mean doing an extra push up, going the extra mile when you feel like stopping. It is challenging yourself to take one more step when you feel like you are at your limit. Simply put, practicing at your edge is choosing to challenge yourself with the desire to see how far you can go.

Staying True to Your Call

One of my greatest desires is to help a person live his or her best life possible. This includes finding one's passion, living one's purpose, and staying true to one's calling. But why? It is my belief that when you live your life based on a sense of call—doing what you love and what you are good at—your life can be transformed from good to great. I once worked a nine-to-five job as an office administrator. I sat at a desk for eight hours per day, five days a week, answering phone calls, entering appropriate company data, and dealing with enquiries from customers. It wasn't very long before I discovered this wasn't my calling. I have since discovered that my calling is to help people live their best life possible through my speaking, coaching, and writing. Quite frankly, I don't think I can do anything else, so I have decided to stay true to my "calling."

The story of Walt Disney exemplifies what is meant by living at the edge of your capability as it relates to staying true to your calling. Having been rejected by numerous film companies that refused to employ him, Mr. Disney used his meager savings to set up a studio in his uncle's garage where he began making animated cartoons. In 1934, Mr. Disney, driven by his calling, took the leap and became the first ever to "create successful full-length animated films including *Snow White, Pinocchio, Fantasia,* and *Bambi*."[113] By staying true to his calling as an animator, Walt Disney continued to live at the edge of his capability, creating theme parks such as Disneyland, Walt Disney World, and EPCOT center. These theme parks have now become the center of fun and enjoyment for children and adults, alike, all over the world.

Like Walt Disney, many of the world's greatest have confessed to having experienced "some kind of force or voice or sense of destiny that has guided them forward."[113] Staying true to your calling will, therefore, act as an impetus to get you out of a place of comfort, as you live at the edge of your capability and push yourself to the next level of your life, career, or profession.

Learn To Embrace Pain

As human beings, we are hard-wired to avoid pain. We

are even conditioned by our parents or guardians as children to avoid pain. They tell us, "Don't do that or don't do this because you will get hurt." The reality is that without pain, we cannot grow. Pain is a physical sensation that signals to us that something is wrong. In essence, pain happens simply to protect you. Whenever you feel pain, your "fight" or "flight" instinct kicks in as the brain lets you know "that what you are doing is wrong, and you need to stop now."[114]

The truth is, not all pain is bad. As a matter of fact, some amount of discomfort is required as a part of a successful training program for athletes. If you are going to build muscles, you have to engage in some amount of strenuous exercise. Furthermore, "for muscle strength to increase, the muscle must see some increase in stress over what it is used to experiencing, and this stress is usually perceived as the 'burn' in muscle during activity. This mild burn is what we call good pain and is the basis of the popular phrase, 'no pain, no gain.'"[115] Any athlete who is serious about winning will have to embrace pain in order to stand on the podium in the end and be crowned a champion.

Embracing pain is also going to be vital for you if you are to exceed yourself, attain greatness, and live the best life you are capable of living. On the path to becoming your best self, bend, don't break! In other words, don't whine, become frustrated, and fall apart. Ask yourself, "What is the worst thing that could happen to me if I embrace the pain?" If the answer isn't death or the end of the world, endure it! Embrace the temporary pain for the joy that is ahead and grow through it as you go through it. The fact is that only through pain can we grow and experience higher levels of joy and achievement possible. Do you think Thomas Edison experienced pain after failing thousands of times on his way to inventing the light bulb? Do you think Roger Bannister experienced pain when he pushed himself to the breaking point and broke the 4-minute mile barrier? Do you think, Edmund Hillary and Tenzing Norgay experienced pain, when they summited Everest? I think they did!

These great pioneers were not different from us. Like them, if you embrace your pain and push yourself beyond what you think you can do, you may just be able to create a similar impact on the world, live a fulfilled life, and leave a legacy behind. The lessons learned from all these pioneers in history, is not that they are better than us, but that "greatness is doable,"[116] because, if something is possible for any other man, it's possible for you, too.

Reflection

WHAT? (WHAT SPOKE TO YOU)

_____
_____
_____
_____
_____
_____
_____

SO WHAT? (YOUR TAKE-AWAY)

_____
_____
_____
_____
_____
_____
_____

NOW WHAT? (YOUR PLAN OF ACTION)

_____
_____
_____
_____
_____
_____
_____

Chapter 9

SO WHERE DO I GO FROM HERE?

"Beginning is half done"
~ Robert Schuller

So what should you do now? What should your next move be? First of all, I hope you enjoyed reading this book as much as I enjoyed writing it. I also hope that you have resolved to use the principles in this book to improve your life so you may live your best life possible.

You've figured out how to exceed yourself and be a success. Now it's time to get it done. Reading was just the beginning, but if you are going to succeed and live your dream, it's going to take continued action to make it happen. You have to stop wishing and start doing.

Without any contradiction, I am convinced that there isn't an individual on the planet who cannot become or do more than she is currently capable of becoming or doing. This means you can be more and you can do more.

The popular saying "You didn't come this far only to come this far" inspires me every day to be better. It is a reminder that I still have a lot of "gas in the tank," that I have the capability of being more than I currently am. Therefore, this book was written to challenge you to be better. Medical science tells us that during the process of fertilization, an average of 100 million sperm are released. They set out on a journey to fertilize the waiting egg, but only one survives this tough trip and ultimately fertilizes the waiting egg.[117] The fact that you are reading this book indicates that you are one out of a 100 million sperm that made it. It means that you have come a long way, not by chance, and that you have what it takes to go even further. Simply put, "you didn't come this far only to come this far."

In Part I of this book, I reminded you that there is greatness within you. I highlighted the fact that the one thing most successful people have in common is hunger. I suggested that if you are going to succeed, you need to get hungry and stay hungry. I also recommended that you program your mind to win, because your subconscious conditioning determines your belief, your belief determines your actions, and your actions determine your outcome. Finally, I encouraged you to unlock your greatness by waking up your innate potential, by updating your self-image, and by believing in yourself.

In Part II, you learned that your dream is possible. I recommended that you tune into your purpose, let your passion fuel you; I also provided you with three ways to get your dream off the launching pad. You were encouraged to believe in your dream, take consistent action, and not stop when you get tired, but only when you are done!

In Part III of this book, you were challenged not to put limits on yourself. You learned that on your path to greatness, you will experience difficulties. I recommended that the way to take on these challenges, and beat the odds is by building resilience through an "I Can," an "I must," and an "I will" approach to life. I also encouraged you to push yourself to the next level. That is, beyond what you think you can do, with the aim of becoming better today that what you were yesterday. I recommended than you practice awareness, raise your standard, and live on the edge of your capability as a way of blowing the lid off your capacity so you may live a phenomenal life.

Thus, what's your next move? Let it be that of taking massive action. Utilize the Cycle of Success formula, as a way of staying on track. In other words, create a plan, take action, review your actions regularly, refine the plan accordingly, and then repeat the process until you get the desired results. Furthermore, seek to be your best at whatever you do and always find a way to exceed expectations.

Life for me has been a journey of twists and turns. Although I was born into poverty to parents who were not able to read and write, and although I was a delinquent teenager and one who failed a lot and struggled to find his way in life, I have finally tasted success. Now it's your turn! I feel privileged to speak at seminars, workshops, retreats, churches, as well as work with individuals and organizations to transform lives. My mission is to help people find their purpose, as well as empowering them to live their best life possible.

I just love the quote from an unknown author who said, "Don't tell me the sky's the limit, when there are footprints on the moon." With that said, now make that decision to unlock your greatness and exceed yourself. Greatness, therefore, awaits you and it is more than doable. My wish for you is that you exceed yourself as you challenge yourself. You deserve the best and you can be the best. There's greatness within you! Exceed Yourself.

Reflection

WHAT? (WHAT SPOKE TO YOU)

_____
_____
_____
_____
_____
_____
_____

SO WHAT? (YOUR TAKE-AWAY)

_____
_____
_____
_____
_____
_____
_____

NOW WHAT? (YOUR PLAN OF ACTION)

_____
_____
_____
_____
_____
_____
_____

Glossary

Appreciative inquiry (AI): A solution-focused approach that seeks to discover and explore the best in people and organizations

Calling: A strong urge toward a career or vocation that brings you joy and fulfillment.

Capacity: The ability to get a job or task done.

Coaching: The process of effecting change in ones life through the candid exploration of ideas with an unbiased and confidential thinker. Simply put, coaching is personal training for the mind.

Competence: Having the skills or ability to do something effectively and successfully.

Conditioning: A process of learning which includes repetitive activities with the intention of influencing behavior.

Conscious mind: The 5 to 10 percent of the mind's capacity where our conscious control of willpower exists.

Deep practice: Engaging in an activity repeatedly while being attentive, hungry, focused, and even desperate.

Expert: Someone who is extraordinarily capable or knowledgeable in his/her field.

Fixed mindset: The belief that one's basic qualities are fixed and cannot change.

Greatness: The ability to identify one's purpose and living it to the best of his/her ability. Service to others is at its core.

Growth mindset: The belief that one's basic qualities and abilities can be developed through hard work and dedication.

Hope: A positive motivational state that accepts reality with an attitude that refuses to give up.

Hunger: A strong desire or craving for something.

Imagining: The process of creating a mental picture of the future with the intent of implementing those creative ideas into practical form.

Mind: The intangible portion of the brain, consisting

of both the conscious and the subconscious mind.

Mindset: The belief and mental attitude of an individual that predetermines his/her response and interpretation to a situation.

Operating system: The software that supports a computer's basic function and is comprised of a set of instructions that tell the computer what to do.

Optimism: Having a positive outlook on life.

Optimist: An individual who expects good things to happen in her life.

Passion: A hunger for what one does or an inner drive to fulfill one's purpose.

Pessimist: Someone who expects bad thing to happen to his/her in life.

Positive Self-talk: The process of overriding past negative programming by replacing it with conscious and more positive directions.

Purpose: A sense of a "calling."

Resilient: Being able to adapt and thrive during difficult life experiences.

Self-actualization: A concept in psychology regarding the motivation to realize one's full potential.

Self-confidence: How secure one feels within oneself and one's abilities.

Self-esteem: The feelings one has about oneself.

Self-image: The view one holds of oneself.

Self-worth: The value one places on oneself.

Standards: The values and behaviors we hold ourselves to.

Strengths: An area in which one is skilled or that thing one is good at.

Subconscious mind: The 90-95 percent of the mind's capacity where most of our influence comes from as it relates to our behavior. This is where our beliefs, values, identity, self-confidence and habits reside.

Success: The progressive realization of a worthy ideal (Earl Nightingale).

Visualize: The process of using one's imagination to create what one wants in life.

Notes

1. The Power of Hunger

[1] Gelderman, 2018.
[2] Great-Quotes.com, n.d., p. 1.
[3] Collins, 2001, p. 20.
[4] The Wealth Choice, 2013.
[5] Steve Jobs Explains the Rules of Success, 2009.
[6] Frankl, 1992, p.76.
[7] Sinek, 2009, pp. 37-42.
[8] Berton Braley Cyber Museum, 2006.

2. The Psychology of Success

[9] Weintraub, 2015, p. 54.
[10] Gallwey, 2008, p. 10.
[11] Gallwey, 2008, p. 16.
[12] Lipton, 2015, p. 122.
[13] Helmstetter, 1982, p. 21.
[14] Lipton, 2015, p. 121.
[15] Allen, 2017, p. 32.
[16] Robbins, 1991, p. 84.
[17] Robbins, 1991, p. 85.
[18] Lipton, 2015, p. 178.
[19] Helmstetter, 1982, p. 72.
[20] Weintraub, 2015, p. 53.

3. Unlock Your Greatness

[21] Epictetus, n.d.
[22] Coyle, 2009, p. 14.
[23] Coyle, 2009, p. 19.
[24] Coyle, 2009, pp. 79-91.
[25] Coyle, 2009, p. 88.
[26] Coyle, 2009, p. 92.
[27] Beckett, 2006.
[28] Coyle, 2009, p. 98.
[29] Maxwell, 2012, p. 219.
[30] Maxwell 2012, p. 219.
[31] Maxwell, 2012, p. 39.
[32] Maltz, 1960, p. 2.
[33] Maltz, 1960, p. 2.
[34] Maxwell, 2012, p. 35.
[35] Brown, 2010.
[36] Campbell, 2015.
[37] Maltz, 1960, p. 2.
[38] BrainyQuote, Winston Churchill Quotes, n.d.
[39] Campbell, 2015.
[40] Gonzalez, 2013, p. 96.
[41] Coyle, 2009, p. 101.

4. Tune Into Your Purpose

[42] Crouch, n.d.
[43] Lienhard, n.d.
[44] Sartwell, 2007, p. 1.
[45] The Definition of Success, 2014.

[46]Hill, 1960, pp. 3-4.
[47]BusinessBalls, n.d.

5. Let Your Passion Fuel You

[48]Sinetar, 1987, p. 9.
[49]Zander & Zander, 2000, p. 113.
[50]The Biography.com, 2018.
[51]Keller, 2013, p. 10.
[52]Keller, 2013, p. 17.
[53]Sartwell, 2007, p. 3.
[54]Greene, 2012, p. 19.
[55]Knapp & Budden, 2018.
[56]Hill, 1960, p. 60.
[57]Dweck, 2006, p. 6.
[58]Malloch, 2009.
[59]WebMD, 2016b.
[60]Howard, 2011.
[61]Gold, 2016.
[62]Usain Bolt – Train like Usain, n.d.
[63]Duckworth, 2016, p. 120.
[64]Ericsson & Pool, 2016, pp. 15-22.
[65]Colvin, 2010, p. 66.

6. Getting Your Dream off The Launching Pad

[66]Meyer, n.d.
[67]Walt Disney Imagination, n.d.
[68]SPACE.com Staff, 2011.

[69] Wolchover, 2012.
[70] Zipes, 2001.\

7. Beating The Odds

[71] Jolie, 2014.
[72] Clarkson, 2011.
[73] Frankl, 1992, p. 76.
[74] Rohn, 2017.
[75] Whitmore, 2009, p. 108.
[76] Siebert, 2005, p. 72.
[77] Snopes, n.d.
[78] Robbins, 1991, p. 273.
[79] Siebert, 2005, p. 109.
[80] Siebert, 2005, p. 109.
[81] Dholakia, 2017.
[82] Self-actualization, n.d.
[83] Sullivan, n.d.
[84] Sullivan, n.d.
[85] Mettler, 2017.
[86] Mettler, 2017.
[87] Dweck, 2006, p. 6.
[88] Dweck, 2006, p. 41.
[89] Kelm, 2015, p. 3.
[90] American Psychological Association, n.d.
[91] Goals Research Study, n.d.
[92] Feinstein, 2014.
[93] BrainyQuote, Napoleon Hill Quotes, n.d.

[94] Hill, 1960, p. 133.
[95] Schuller, 1984.
[96] Schuller, 1997.
[97] Duckworth, 2016, p. 187.
[98] Hill, 1960, p. 134.
[99] Pink, 2009, p. 127.

8. Push Yourself To The Next Level
[100] Hoobyar & Dotz, 2013, p. 9.
[101] Greene, 2012, p. 29.
[102] Hoobyar & Dotz, 2013, p. 53.
[103] Team Tony, n.d.
[104] Greene, 2012, p. 64.
[105] Maxwell, 2017, p. 38.
[106] Maxwell, 2017, p. 41.
[107] Loehr and Schwartz, 2003, p. 4.
[108] Maxwell, 2017, p. 57.
[109] Maxwell, 2017, p. 92.
[110] Collins, 2001, p. 1.
[111] Colvin, 2010, p. 90.
[112] Collins, 2001, p. 195.
[113] Greene, 2012, p. 25.
[114] Rodriguez, 2013.
[115] McFarland & Cosgarea, n.d.
[116] Duckworth, 2016, p. 38.

9. So Where Do I Go From Here?
[117] WebMD, 2016a.

Bibliography

Allen, J. (2017). *As a man thinketh*: Original 1902 edition. Scotts Valley, CA: CreateSpace.

American Psychological Association. (n.d.). The road to resilience [Website]. Retrieved from http://www.apa.org/helpcenter/road-resilience.aspx

Beckett, S. (2006, March). The Economist. Try again. *Fail again. Fail better*. Retrieved from https://www.economist.com/node/5624852.

Berton Braley Cyber Museum. (2006. June 13). Success. Retrieved from https://www .bertonbraley.com/

The Biography.com [Website]. (2018, January 18). *Michael Jordan Biography*. Retrieved from https://www.biography.com/people/michael-jordan-9358066

BrainyQuote. (n.d.). Napoleon Hill Quotes [Webpage]. Retrieved from https://www .brainyquote.com/quotes/napoleon_hill_152875

BrainyQuote. (n.d.). Winston Churchill Quotes [Webpage]. Retrieved from https://www .brainyquote.com/quotes/winston_churchill_103739.

Brown, B. (2010). *The gift of imperfection: Let go of who you think you're supposed to be and embrace who you are.* Center City, MN: Hazelden.

Burns, D. (1993). Ten days to self-esteem. New York, NY: HarperCollins.

BusinessBalls. (n.d.). Conscious competence learning model [Webpage]. Retrieved from https://www.businessballs.com/self-awareness/conscious-competence-learning-model-63/

Campbell, P. (2015, December). *Why you should celebrate everything.* Retrieved from https://www.psychologytoday.com/ca/blog/imperfect-spirituality/201512/why-you-should-celebrate-everything.

Clarkson, K. (2011, December). Kelly Clarkson - *Stronger (What Doesn't Kill You)* [Video file]. Retrieved from https://www.youtube.com/watch?v=Xn676-fLq7I&feature=youtu.be

Collins, J. (2001). Good to great. New York, NY: HarperCollins.

Colvin, G. (2010). *Talent is over-rated.* New York, NY: Penguin.

Coyle, D. (2009). *The talent code: Greatness isn't born. It's grown. Here's how.* New York, NY: Bantam Dell.

Crouch, T. D. (n.d.). Samuel Pierpont Langley: America Engineer. *In Encyclopedia Britannica.* Retrieved from https://www.britannica.com/biography/Samuel-Pierpont-Langley

The Definition of Success. (2014, November). *Earl Nightingale:* The strangest secret (1950) [Video file]. Retrieved from https://www.youtube.com/watch?v=HFV9IX_O3ho

Dholakia, U. (2017, February). What's the Difference Between Optimism and Hope? *Psychology Today.* Retrieved from https://www.psychologytoday.com/ca/blog/the-science-behind-behavior/201702/whats-the-difference-between-optimism-and-hope.

Duckworth, A. (2016). Grit: *The power of passion and perseverance.* Toronto, ON: HarperCollins.

Dweck, C. S. (2006). Mindset: *The new psychology of success.* New York, NY: Ballantine Books.

Epictetus. (n.d.). AZ Quotes [Website]. Retrieved from http://www.azquotes.com/quote/ 798097.

Ericsson, A., & Pool, R. (2016). *Peak: Secrets from the new science of expertise*. London, England: Bodley Head.

Feinstein, A. (2014, April). Why you should be writing down your goals. *Forbes*. Retrieved from http://www.forbes.com/sites/85broads/2014/04/08/why-you-should-be-writing-down-your-goals/.

Frankl, V. E. (1992). Man's search for meaning. Boston, MA: Beacon Press.

Gallwey, W, T. (2008). The inner game of tennis. New York, NY: Random House.

Gelderman, C. W. (2018, March). *Henry Ford*. Retrieved from https://www.britannica .com/biography/Henry-Ford

Goals Research Study [Webpage]. (n.d.). Retrieved from https://www.dominican.edu/ academics/lae/undergraduate-programs/psych/faculty/assets-gail-matthews/ researchsummary2.pdf

Gold, J. (2016, May). *Usain Bolt training routine:* Diet plan and tips. Retrieved from http://www.borntoworkout.com/usain-bolt-training-routine-diet-plan-tips/.

Gonzalez, D. C. (2013). *The art of mental training*. N.p: GonzoLane Media.

Great-Quotes.com [Website]. (n.d.). Henry Ford Quotes. Retrieved from http://www.great-quotes.com/quotes/author/Henry/Ford

Greene, R. (2012). *Mastery*. New York, NY: Penguin.

Helmstetter, S. (1982). *What to say when you talk to yourself*. New York, NY: Pocket Books.

Hill, N. (1960). *Think and grow rich*. New York, NY: Random House.

Hoobyar, T., & Dotz, T. (2013). NLP: *The essential guide*. New York, NY: HarperCollins.

Howard, D. (2011, November). *The mag: Q & A with Usain Bolt*. Retrieved from http://www.espn.com/olympics/story/_/id/7294360/olympics-usain-bolt-being-fastest-man-world-espn-magazine.

Jolie, A. (Director), Jolie, A., Townsend, C., Baer, M., & Stoff, E. (Producers). (2014, December). *Unbroken*. United States: Universal Pictures & Legendary Pictures.

Keller, G. (2013). *The one thing: The surprisingly simple truth behind extraordinary results.* Austin, TX: Bard Press.

Kelm, J. B. (2015). *Appreciative living: The principles of appreciative inquiry in persona.* Charleston, SC: Venet.

Knapp. R. L., & Budden, J. M. (2018, May 23). Ludwig Van Beethoven: German composer. *In Encyclopedia Britannica.* Retrieved from https://www.britannica.com/biography/Ludwig-van-Beethoven/Approaching-deafness

Lienhard, J. H. (n.d.). Wright and Langley [Webpage]. *Engines of our ingenuity.* Retrieved from http://www.uh.edu/engines/epi32.htm

Lipton, B. H. (2015). *The biology of belief.* New York, NY: Hay House.

Loehr, J., & Schwartz, T. (2003). *The power of full engagement.* New York, NY: Free Press.

Malloch, D. (2009). *Be the best of whatever you are.* Retrieved from http://bachlund.org/ Be_the_best_of_whatever_you_are.htm

Maltz, M. (1960). *Psycho-Cybernetics.* Englewood Cliffs, NJ: Prentice-Hall.

Maxwell, J. C. (2012). *The 15 invaluable laws of growth.* New York, NY: Yates & Yates.

Maxwell, J. C. (2017). *No limits: Blow the cap off your capacity.* New York, NY: Hachette Book Group.

McFarland, E. G., & Cosgarea, A. (n.d.). 'Good pain' versus 'bad pain' for athletes. *Johns Hopkins Medicine.* Retrieved from https://www.hopkinsmedicine.org/orthopaedic-surgery/about-us/ask-the-experts/pain.html

Mettler, K. (2017, January 11). Obama's 'Yes We Can' almost didn't happen. You can thank Michelle for saving it. *Washington Post.* Retrieved from https://www.washingtonpost.com/news/morning-mix/wp/2017/01/11/obamas-yes-we-can-thank-michelle-for-that/?noredirect=on&utm_term=.e499c7c04eb1.

Meyer, P. J. (n.d.). *Awards and recognition.* Retrieved from http://pauljmeyer.com/the-legacy/awards-recognition/

Pink, D. H. (2009). *Drive: The surprising truth about what motivates us.* New York, NY: Riverhead Books

Robbins, A. (1991). *Awaken the giant within.* New York, NY: Free Press.

Rodriguez, D. (2013, August). Why do we feel pain? *Everyday Health* [Website]. Retrieved from https://www.everydayhealth.com/pain-management/how-pain-works.aspx

Rohn. J. (2017, June). *10 things you must improve everyday to get whatever you want* [Video file]. Retrieved from https://m.youtube.com/watch?v=KWxTbSAqmrE.

Sartwell, M. (2007). *Napolean Hill's key to success: The 17 principles of personal achievement.* New York, NY: Penguin.

Schuller, R. (1984). *Tough times don't last, but tough people do.* New York, NY: Bantam Books.

Schuller, R. (1997). *If it's going to be, it's up to me.* New York, NY: HarperCollins.

Self-actualization. (n.d.). *In Business Dictionary.* Retrieved from http://www.businessdictionary.com/definition/self-actualization.html

Siebert, A. (2005). *The resiliency advantage.* San Francisco, CA: Barrett-Koehler.

Sinek, S. (2009). *Start with why.* New York, NY: Penguin.

Sinetar, M. (1987). *Do what you love, the money will follow.* New York, NY: Dell.

Snopes. (n.d.). Abraham Lincoln and failure [Webpage]. Retrieved from https://www.snopes.com/fact-check/abraham-lincoln-failure/

SPACE.com Staff. (2011, May 25). May 25, 1961: JFK's moon shot speech to Congress [Webpage]. Retrieved from https://www.space.com/11772-president-kennedy-historic-speech-moon-space.html/

Steve Jobs Explains the Rules of Success [Video file]. (2009, September). Retrieved from https://m.youtube.com/watch?v=KuNQgln6TL0

Sullivan, E. (n.d.). Self-actualization. *In Encyclopedia Britannica.* Retrieved from https://www.britannica.com/science/self-actualization.

Team Tony. (n.d.). How to raise your standards [Webpage]. Retrieved from https://www.tonyrobbins.com/mind-meaning/how-to-raise-your-standards/

Usain Bolt – Train like Usain [Video file]. (n.d.). Retrieved from https://www.youtube.com/watch?v=0b_KrJf9uic

Walt Disney Imagination. (n.d.). *About Imagineering* [Website]. Retrieved from https://disneyimaginations.com/about-imaginations/about-imagineering/

The Wealth Choice [Video file]. (2013, September). Retrieved from https://m.youtube.com/watch?v=UPbNFbvKVww

WebMD. (2016a). Sperm FAQ [Webpage]. Retrieved from https://www.webmd.com/ infertility-and-reproduction/guide/sperm-and-semen-faq#1

WebMD. (2016b). What is scoliosis and what causes it? [Webpage]. Retrieved from https://www.webmd.com/back-pain/causes-scoliosis#1

Weintraub, P. (2015, May 4). The voice of reason. Psychology Today, 54.

Whitmore, J. (2009). *Coaching for performance* (4th ed.). Boston, MA: Brealey.

Wolchover, N. (2012, August). 'One small step for man': Was Neil Armstrong misquoted? In *Space.com* [Website]. Retrieved from https://www.space.com/17307-neil-armstrong-one-small-step-quote.html.

Zander, R., & Zander, B. (2000). *The art of possibility:* Transforming professional and personal life. Cambridge, MA: Harvard Business School Press.

Zipes, D. P. (2001, December). President's page: "The Great End Of Life Is Not Knowledge But Action."— Thomas Henry Huxley (1825–95). *Journal of the American College of Cardiology.* Retrieved from http://www.onlinejacc.org/ content/38/7/2088.

About the Author

Floyd S. Spence, is a life strategist, speaker and coach with expertise in Mindset and the Psychology of Success. He is the founder and CEO of Live Full Coaching and Consulting, a company that specializes in the training and development of individuals and organizations. Dr. Floyd is also the author of the book *Made To Love You: The Art of Romantic Love In Marriage* and is driven by the mantra, "There's Greatness Within You." He currently resides in Toronto, Ontario, Canada, but considers the world his oyster. Dr. Floyd can be reached at drfloyd@floydspence.com for consultation and speaking engagements.

CONNECT WITH
DR. FLOYD

To have Dr. Floyd speak at your event or organization about the principles found in Exceed Yourself, or other success insights, email speak@floydspence.com.

For more information about Dr. Floyd, Visit:
Website: Floydspence.com
Twitter: @drfloydspence
Facebook: Drfloydspence

FLOYD S. SPENCE

MADE TO LOVE YOU

THE ART OF ROMANTIC LOVE IN MARRIAGE

www.ingramcontent.com/pod-product-compliance
Lightning Source LLC
Chambersburg PA
CBHW060134100426
42744CB00007B/779